W9-BKH-440

The Guide
to Understanding
Financial Statements

The Guide to Understanding Financial Statements

A revised edition of
Financial Statements of Small Business

S. B. COSTALES

McGRAW-HILL BOOK COMPANY
New York St. Louis San Francisco Auckland Bogotá Düsseldorf
London Madrid Mexico Montreal
New Delhi Panama Paris São Paulo
Singapore Sydney Tokyo Toronto

#4493121

2-90

Library of Congress Cataloging in Publication Data

Costales, S B
   The guide to understanding financial statements.

   Includes index.
   1. Financial statements.   I. Title.
HF5681.B2C597   1979   657'.3   78-26521
ISBN 0-07-013190-2

11 12 13 14 15 DODO 8 9

The editor for this book was Kiril Sokoloff
and the production supervisor was Teresa F. Leaden.

Printed and bound by R. R. Donnelley & Sons Company.

CONTENTS

PREFACE

In America, there is a surprising lack of knowledge of business financial statements—a lack which exists most significantly among owners of small and medium-sized businesses. This observation has been echoed by certified public accountants, bank loan officers, and many people in business themselves, and after thirty years of experience as a commercial bank loan officer, I am convinced that it is true.

At the latest Dun and Bradstreet count, there were 3 million manufacturers, wholesalers, and retailers in active business in the United States, not including many more hundreds of thousands engaged in consumer services. All these people are struggling to gather in enough income to pay bills, taxes, expenses, and salaries—and still end up each year with a reasonable net profit. With these facts in mind, it is alarming to think that a large number of people may not completely understand their financial condition.

Why is it that so many of us have not studied and do not understand the basic element in our economic profit system—the operation of a business organization?

Consider another increasingly important element in our national economy—the feverish buying and selling of stocks on Wall Street. We have the New York Stock Exchange, the American Stock Exchange, the so-called "over-the-counter" securities not specifically listed on any exchange but bought and sold by most brokers, and the many local stock exchanges in our principal cities. At times, close to 20 million shares are traded in one day on the New York exchange alone, and millions more shares move in the other securities outlets.

In recent years thousands of people have become part of America's corporate structure by the purchase of a single stock certificate. And yet how many of them can even partially appraise the value of a purchase? How many people who have bought stock on tips from so-called "reliable sources" would be able to evaluate an accurate financial statement pertaining to a purchase?

The fact that all of us are involved to varying degrees in the profit system makes a preliminary study of that system necessary. In examining the search for business profits, we will consider the relentless battle with unfair competition, price fluctuations, changes in products and methods, government regulations, income taxes, and labor problems.

In addition to these and other obstacles, economic recessions appear to come upon us every two or three years as inventories build up ahead of the demand for goods, and the ensuing digestive process results in unemployment. Directly after World War II, almost anyone could succeed in business as pent-up demand for scarce consumer products created unprecedented prosperity throughout the country. However, since about 1957, our economy has undergone two recessions. Since then, the number of business concerns bidding for the consumer dollar has increased and the battle for economic existence has intensified. A better understanding of our financial selves is more than ever a requisite if we are to survive in business.

There should be no mystery about commercial financial statements. This volume will present an uncomplicated interpretation and analysis of the financial condition of the small commercial enterprise. Small and medium-sized business are the concern here rather than multimillion dollar corporations, which represent a small percentage of all businesses.

An additional chapter has been included in this edition. It concerns an actual case history of a business which started off on the worst possible basis—with little capital stock and substantial bank loans. The chapter should serve as a warning to people starting a business venture overburdened with debt.

The book as a whole strives to present the importance of financial statements in forming and maintaining a successful business.

S. B. Costales

The Guide
to Understanding
Financial Statements

CHAPTER I

HISTORICAL DEVELOPMENT OF FINANCIAL STATEMENTS

Certainly, one of the very first to make a beginning was Normand Smith — craftsman and hand maker of fine saddles, harnesses, buckskin clothing and sundry leather goods. On August 9th in the year 1794, he proclaimed to his neighbors that certain goods were for sale and could be inspected and purchased in his shop in the City of Hartford, Connecticut. The venture prospered and continued under the sole management of his descendants until 1885 when George Worthington was taken in as a partner. At this writing, the business is known as the Smith-Worthington Saddlery Company, manufacturing the same products as in 1794, and its financial condition continues strong.

It is apparent that no books or financial records were maintained in the beginning. However, I have been privileged to examine such ledgers and books of account that have survived the years back to August 1, 1818 (forty-three years before The Civil War). On that wonderful day, a hundred and fifty-one years ago, one Levi Morgan, being of good credit and reputation, did "take from stock" two Best Englishman Saddles at $6.50 each. Levi continued to purchase a variety of leather goods, and from time to time, it was written in beautiful but long forgotten penmanship, he made certain cash payments on account. Finally, on January 2, 1820, it was written, "Received payment in full by their account and by cash."

There is an unfortunate gap in the records from 1818 to 1856, but during those years some bookkeeping progress was apparently made as indicated by an Inventory Ledger dated June 7, 1856. Also, a "Wages for Labor" book was maintained listing the number of hours of labor and total pay for each worker. It was written that one Elias Bland was paid $24 for 80 hours work, or 30¢ per hour. One William Lane labored 60 hours and received a total of $9, or 15¢ per hour. Could Billy Lane have been just a child?

And so it was that only brief and aimless attention was given to the keeping of records in those early days of American commerce. In fact, commercial banks through the 1800's made loans on the basis of several endorsers, or guarantors, who promised to pay the note if the maker defaulted on his obligation to the bank. There appeared to be no need for a financial statement revealing assets and debts of the borrower as long as his guarantors were gentlemen of good character and reputation.

However, even then, a revolutionary event in American history was on its way to change all this, and touch the economic lives of us all with ever increasing force from year to year. On October 3, 1913, President Woodrow Wilson put his signature on The Sixteenth Amendment to The Federal Constitution empowering Congress "to lay and collect taxes on incomes, from whatever sources derived, without apportionment among the several states, and without regard to any census." Now, for the first time, all the Normand Smiths throughout the country found that they had an uninvited partner — The United States Government — a partner most interested in the size of taxable business profits.

It is believed that the first Accountants came to our young Country from England, having been engaged to inspect and investigate British interests here.[1] These early financial visitors must have sensed the exciting opportunity for their profession in our turbulent, bursting economic frontier, and in 1881 Candor and Carnes advertised themselves as "Expert Accountants." Thus, the profession of accountancy made a feeble beginning and assumed a position of increasing importance in the business scene. Gradually, bookkeeping procedures

---

[1] *From "The Genesis of 14 Important Ratios," by Roy Foulke,*
Dun and Bradstreet, Inc.

2

and the formula of debits and credits evolved into our present day mathematical exactness of The Three Principal Forms of Financial Statements:

The Balance Sheet

The Profit and Loss Statement

The Reconcilation of Net Worth Statement

Undoubtedly the Federal Income Tax Law was most responsible for the birth of Financial Statements in this country. However, the short-lived Money Panic in 1920, and certainly the awesome Great Depression of the 1930's, badly shook the confidence of the banks in names and reputations alone. After millions of dollars of uncollectible bank loans were charged off, new borrowers, you may be sure, were asked certain questions regarding their personal holdings (assets) and their liabilities (debts).

So, in the early 1900's, businessmen were literally forced to employ outside accountants to prepare financial statements for the inspection of The Federal Government, and to facilitate the vital flow of bank credit into their organizations.

Finally, following the Stock Market Crash in 1929, one other development of the 1930's was the advent of The Securities and Exchange Commission which was empowered to look, often with a critical eye, into the financial condition of any corporation offering its Capital Stock to the public. Obviously, very detailed financial reports had to be prepared, and the science of good accountancy now has reached a stage of development which reveals every financial nook and corner of a business enterprise.

For an understanding, we need to grasp a relatively few accounting principals and formulae which will be outlined in the following pages. The simplicity of the next few Chapters may be boring to the initiated, but simplicity is a requirement for the beginner. We invite you to persevere to Chapters which analyze actual Financial Statements.

We stress again that these Statements deal with **Small** Business, but the same principles and concepts can be applied to very **Large Corporations.**

CHAPTER II

THE NATURE OF BUSINESS ORGANIZATIONS

There are basically only three types of commercial organizations — Proprietorship (Sole Owner), Partnership (two or more partners), and Corporation (owned by stockholders). Each of these has its advantages and each its disadvantages, principally from the angle of income taxes and personal liability. In deciding which is most beneficial, an Accountant can calculate the income tax advantages in each case, and a Lawyer might advise, for instance, that the business should be operated as a corporation after considering all the circumstances. In any event, no one should attempt to venture into the business world on his own without the confidential services of an Accountant and a Lawyer.

PROPRIETORSHIP:

This is the simplest form of business organization in which only one individual person owns all the assets, on the favorable side, but the sole owner is also personally liable for all debts owed by his business. If he is successful, he and he alone is entitled to all the profits. But, if financial trouble comes and he is unable to pay his bills, creditors may attach his home, his auto, his bank account, or any other personal assets that can be found.

Perhaps psychological, but none the less strong, is the urge "to be my own boss," and for many people this is a definite advantage of a proprietorship. You sink or swim on your own decisions, and no one has the right to tell you what to do! This is ideal, just as long as the batting average of your judgment turns out to be reasonably high.

Of course, a business conducted as a Proprietorship is completely dependent upon the good health and even the very life of the Owner. In the event of death, all contracts become null and void, and the business literally ceases to exist with all manner of resulting problems.

5

In the case of a Partnership or Corporation, the business could go on as usual through the benefits of a properly planned life insurance program.

Finally, a Proprietor must pay an income tax on the entire amount of his net profit, regardless of the amount he draws for himself. There is little latitude for lawful maneuvering in this tax problem and, again, one needs the advice of an expert accountant. To sum up the nature of a Proprietorship:

Advantages	Disadvantages
Enjoyment of all profit.	All personal assets
Make own decisions.	subject to Liability.
	Limited to life of owner.
	Entire profit is taxed.

PARTNERSHIP:

The Uniform Partnership Act, now adopted by many States, defines a Partnership as "an association of two or more persons to carry on as co-owners a business for profit." In reality, the great majority of partnerships are composed of just two persons, each having an equal voice in the management and each sharing equally in the profits. A specific Partnership Agreement, drawn by a Lawyer, is vitally important here to avoid any misunderstandings as to the rights and duties of each partner. Two advantages of a Partnership are perhaps the doubling of capital funds to operate an expanding business, and possibly a more balanced management.

By and large in most cases, the two partners share alike in the profits and each has an equal voice in making decisions — and there's the rub. In this respect alone, a fifty-fifty association of two partners can be the least desirable of the three forms of business organizations. In the event of disagreement, an absolute stalemate is reached and their business suffers. Assume that one partner is convinced that a branch store should be opened in another, growing section of town, but the other partner is just as convinced that this move would be a great mistake. The result — nothing happens — the seeds of distrust and of future disagreements have been planted.

One important and potentially dangerous characteristic of a Partnership is that one partner has the legal power to bind the other in any ordinary transactions necessary for the conduct of the business. In other words, either partner alone can negotiate a bank loan, buy materials, or purchase equipment and the Partnership itself is liable for payment of these normal transactions.

Also, personal liability for the payment of Partnership debts remains a feature of this type of business organization. If financial trouble comes, the partners' homes, autos, bank accounts, etc., may be attached by dissatisfied creditors.

Again death cancels all contracts and unless the surviving partner, or the business itself, has adequate funds to purchase the deceased's interest in the firm, the company would simply crumble out of existence. Any Partnership of appreciable size should purchase a Life Insurance Program supervised by its accountant and insurance agent. Each partner would be named the beneficiary in the life insurance policy of the other, so that, in the event of the death of either, sufficient cash would be available to buy out the deceased's interest without financial strain on the survivor. To sum up the nature of A Partnership:

Advantages	Disadvantages
Double operating capital.	Personal liability.
Possibly a more balanced	Bound by each others
management.	commitments.
	Life of a partnership is
	limited without insurance.

CORPORATION:

During May in the year 1792 at Hartford, Connecticut, the Governor, the Council, and the House of Representatives passed an Act to incorporate "The Hartford Bank." Capital stock was "to consist of $100,000 to be divided into 250 shares, each share being $400." Thus began one of the first commercial banks in early America. From that modest beginning of $100,000 in Capital Stock, the "Old Hartford Bank" today now has accumulated Total Assets of more than one billion dollars ($1,045,206,039). The popularity of the corporate structure has grown through the years, and today there are more than 23,000 corporations doing business in the State of Connecticut alone.

An historical definition of a corporation — "Any separate body consisting of one or more individuals treated by the law as a unit, and especially with the right to perpetual succession." A Corporation is authorized and regulated by the laws of the various States; it must stay within the limits of its asserted functional purpose (e.g., manu-

7

facture shoes and nothing else); and it can act only through Directors and Officers, properly elected by its Stockholders who provide the original Capital funds.

At the time of its birth, a corporation financial statement would report the dollar amount of its original paid in Capital Stock under Liabilities ($100,000 in the case of The Hartford Bank). As, and if, net profits are earned, a sister item named "Surplus" is created which accumulates all net profit after income taxes and dividends paid to stockholders. The two related items of Capital Stock and Surplus are quite properly listed as Liabilities because the corporation literally **owes** these amounts of money to its stockholders — first on account of shareholders' original investment, and second, the corporation owes its stockholders the profits made on their investment.

Perhaps the greatest advantage of a Corporation is its perpetual existence. Directors and Officers may retire, or die, but the Corporate entity goes on under the direction of new managers properly elected as replacements.

Equally important to the owners of a corporation is the extremely limited nature of their personal liability for corporate acts and debts. Technically, a stockholder is liable up to the dollar amount of his stockholdings, but very rarely, if ever, is he called upon to make good the debts of the corporation.

Unlike the fifty-fifty partnership stalemate, it is often possible for one group of several stockholders, who hold similar views and convictions, to band together in the voting on company decisions and policies. In this manner of control, management could become more dynamic, more purposeful, and progressive.

Finally, the corporate structure provides for the acquisition of additional capital funds without necessarily changing the majority stock control of the founders. At the time of incorporation, application is made to the State for permission to have $200,000 of stock authorized but, let us say, only $150,000 is actually required to start the business. As progress is made and profits reported, the stock then becomes attractive to capital investors who might purchase and be issued an additional $25,000 in stock certificates. Thus, company working capital is enlarged to handle an expanding volume of business.

One traditional objection to the corporate form of organization is the burden of so called "double taxation." The great majority of business corporations are small in size and are principally owned by one or two families. The Officers, usually the owners, are paid a salary by the company and a personal tax must be paid on that amount of income each year. In addition, the corporation's own net profit for the year is also taxed resulting in the perennial but often legitimate cry of "double taxation."

The Internal Revenue Service recently has been empowered to offer some relief in this tax problem to small business corporations. Again, we repeat, consult with your accountant — there may be a real saving of profit in this new income tax angle. To sum up the nature of a Corporation:

Advantages	Disadvantages
Perpetual existence.	Restricted by law to func-
Very limited stockholder's	tions.
liability.	Possible double taxation.
More dynamic management.	
Access to more capital funds.	

FOUR BASIC TYPES OF BUSINESS

Manufacturing
Wholesale
Retail
Services

The above listing is deliberate, and is intended to illustrate the traditional flow of goods and materials from their source, the manufacturer, to the wholesale distributor, then to the eventual consumer outlet, the retailer. Service organizations (such as bus lines, taxi companies, theatres, tailors and dry cleaners, etc.) do not sell merchandise, but offer only their services. In other respects, service organizations are much like retailers — they are retailers of a service to the consumer.

MANUFACTURING:

The actual production of merchandise and materials is the most complex and hazardous of all the four types of business ventures.

1. First, there must be a substantial investment in Fixed Assets — machinery, equipment, and a factory building. A miscalculation here, or the excessive purchase of unnecessary Fixed Assets, could put a heavy strain on cash needed for working capital.

2. Raw Materials, going into the manufacture of the finished product, must be purchased in the right quantity and the right price. For instance, if we are in an upward, inflationary phase of the business cycle, there is always the temptation to purchase today more material than we actually need because we feel sure that the cost for the same material will go up tomorrow. As a matter of fact, this very common purchasing policy amongst businessmen throughout the country often eventually leads to a general business recession, as we realize that we have purchased inventory too far beyond the real requirements of our sales volume. Then begins a period of so-called "inventory liquidation to reduce stocks to a point more in line with sales." This classic statement by management simply means that we are slowing down our manufacturing process and laying off some workers until we have digested a good part of our inventory.

3. The Labor Problem is the most troublesome of all for the harassed manufacturer. The cost of labor is his largest expense item, and the aggregate dollar amount inches up year after year. The cost of labor simply must be added into the selling price of the manufacturer's product in a competitive market. Yet, the Labor Union wage scale, plus fringe benefits, must be met in order to keep machines humming.

One manufacturer of cutting tools employs 250 workers to turn out a sales volume of $2,000,000 per year.

4. Continually strive for more efficient methods of manufacture to reduce operating costs. Try to keep at least abreast of competitors through research and the development of new products.

5. Plan on surrendering from 25% to 40% of net profit for Federal Income Taxes.

6. In addition to all the foregoing, struggle to have enough profit left over to justify the payment of reasonable dividends to stockholders.

7. Finally, even after paying dividends, retain in Surplus a fair amount of profit needed to carry on the business.

WHOLESALE:

Products of manufacturers are purchased by wholesale companies located in larger cities across the country. Each operates in a fairly limited territory selling merchandise to hundreds of small retail stores in its area. The outstanding feature of the wholesaler is the traditionally small margin of profit, so that sales volume must be as large as possible, but expenses must be kept to a minimum. By going farther afield to get more sales, expenses would simply increase to the point of the "law of diminishing returns."

1. Fortunately, then, the wholesaler requires a much smaller investment in Fixed Assets which are usually represented by a warehouse and office building (or he could rent from others) office equipment, and delivery trucks.

2. Labor costs are lower than in manufacturing, and again, this is most fortunate in view of the narrow profit margin. One wholesaler of drugs and liquors employs only 80 people and yet does an annual sales volume of $7,000,000.

3. The wholesaler does have a definite Credit Problem. Whereas the manufacturer deals with a relatively few, well established firms, the selling of merchandise on 30 day credit terms to hundreds of small retail stores is a risky business. Again, in view of the narrow profit margin in wholesaling, the over liberal and easy granting of credit to retailers could be fatal.

4. Since a large sales volume is required by a wholesaler, this means that large inventories of merchandise must also be maintained to satisfy the varied needs of retail customers. The fine point of judgment here is to carry enough goods to meet customers' demands, yet keep a proper inventory balance and avoid over-stocking.

RETAIL:

Here is the final outlet of merchandise to the consumer, with its own peculiarities and risks.

1. The retailer must "put up a good front," which too often means a heavy investment in modern store fixtures, counters, expensive rugs, interior decorating, exterior neon signs, and a variety of other eye-catching tinsel. Unfortunately, much of all this is often accomplished by a moderate cash down payment leaving a substantial balance to be paid over a period of several years and net profits must be sufficient to carry this and other burdens of debt.

2. Experienced judgement in buying merchandise for a retail store can mean the difference between economic life or death. Cer-

tainly, no one can do business from an empty wagon, but there is often an over-eagerness to have a large and varied stock of goods on hand to tempt the customer. Periodically, wholesalers will offer "specials" to the retailer—buy now in large quantities and get a special discount off the regular price. The well-heeled store owner can afford to take advantage of these profitable offers which give him a definite edge over his under-capitalized competitors. But for most merchants struggling along with limited cash, the nibbling at the "discount" bait simply pushes him deeper in debt.

3. One very common method of generating retail sales is to offer easy, painless credit terms—"buy now, pay later." Of course, this creates a never ending Credit Problem as consumers are encouraged and almost driven to overload themselves with personal debts. Fortunately, most charge accounts are relatively small in dollars, so that the law of averages works to the benefit of the retailer.

4. The selection of a location for a store is usually an expensive venture. Very simply, the choicest spots are always in the "high rent district." It would not be uncommon to find a retailer paying rent equal to 5% or 6% of his annual sales volume. If sales were $200,000 per year, rental costs could be $10,000 to $12,000 per year, a heavy weight to bear in the competitive race.

Sales personnel must be paid wages commensurate with others in the same area, not to mention the ever present fringe benefits.

One unique and very material expense item in retailing is the constant necessity for Advertising. A certain amount of publicity is undoubtedly needed, and the fine point of business judgement is to avoid excessive advertising expense.

5. In the face of the foregoing, the relatively large profit markup in retail businesses should not be so shocking to the consuming public. Any material cutting of retail prices could be the beginning of the end for the average over-burdened store owner. He must maintain an adequate gross profit margin in the selling price of his mechandise to stay alive.

In Chapter III we begin a gentle approach to Financial Statements themselves. As between the types and forms of commercial organizations discussed in this Chapter, there are a few important differences in the Financial Statements of each business category. These variances will be pointed out in separate sections of the chapters dealing with three financial statements—**The Balance Sheet, The Profit and Loss Statement,** and **The Reconciliation of Net Worth Statement.**

QUESTIONS ON CHAPTER II:

1. Describe the characteristics of (1) a Proprietorship, (2) a Partnership, and (3) a Corporation.

2. What are the advantages and disadvantages of each of the above?

3. Outline the special peculiarities and problems in the three "Basic Types of Business Organizations" — Manufacturing, Wholesale, and Retail.

CHAPTER III

THE BALANCE SHEET

The Balance Sheet is a listing of all Assets (ownership of any real, or tangible items which may be used to pay debts) in one column to the left of a page, and a listing of all liabilities (all debts presently outstanding) to the right. The mathematical difference between the two is called Net Worth.

ASSETS		LIABILITIES	
Cash	$ 5,000	Accounts Payable	$ 8,000
Accounts Receivable ...	10,000	Bank Loan Payable	5,000
Inventory	15,000		
Real Estate	25,000	Real Estate Mortgage .	10,000
Trucks	5,000	Net Worth	37,000
Total Assets	**$60,000**	**Total Liabilities**	**$60,000**

Thus Net Worth is not only the "balancing factor," which makes Total Assets balance with or equal to Total Liabilities, but Net Worth also reveals the dollar amount of the owner's interest, or equity, in his business. Theoretically, if the owner could sell today all his assets for $60,000 cash, he could pay off all his debts of $23,000 and end up with $37,000 cash for himself.

Terminology of Balance Sheet Items:

ASSETS

CASH — on hand in the till or on deposit in a bank.

ACCOUNTS RECEIVABLE — with the exception of Discount Houses, and a very few others, practically all sales of merchandise and products are made on open account credit — delivery of the goods now, and payment expected within the next 30 to 60 days. The asset item of Accounts Receivable is a grand total of all money owed to the business and still unpaid as of the date of the Balance Sheet.

INVENTORY — this is the term for merchandise, stock of goods on hand for sale, or products for sale in the case of a manufacturer.

FIXED ASSETS — Also known as Slow Assets — these are such items as Real Estate (Land and Buildings), Machinery, Trucks, Equipment and Store Fixtures. Under this classification would also appear perhaps doubtful assets, such as a Slow Account Receivable which has been reduced gradually but has been on the books for almost a year or more; an outside speculative investment is some land; the purchase of stock in another company, which probably could not be sold quickly for cash; etc.

OTHER ASSETS — these are of a miscellaneous nature and will be discussed as they arise in Statement Studies later on.

LIABILITIES

ACCOUNTS PAYABLE — the counterpart of accounts receivable. This is the grand total of all money owed by the business to others on account of merchandise or materials purchased, perhaps 30 days previous and due for payment at the date of the Balance Sheet.

BANK LOAN PAYABLE — cash obtained from a commercial bank on a promissory note signed by the owner and due for payment perhaps within the next 90 days.

LONG TERM LIABILITIES — such as a Real Estate Mortgage, or a bank loan not due for payment until one year after date of the Statement.

OTHER LIABILITIES — these include such imminent obligations as reserve for income tax (if a corporation), rent due shortly, employee Social Security Taxes Withheld, etc., and will be discussed as they arise in Statement Studies later on.

THE DUAL CHARACTER OF THE BALANCE SHEET

Yes, the Balance Sheet has two faces, and should be split into two theoretically separate sections. The upper part of Assets contains **only** those Assets which are self liquidating into cash and the lower part contains **only** those Assets which are used by and in the business (not intended to revolve into cash), such as Real Estate, Machinery, or Store Fixtures. This later sub-classification would also include slow receivables, outside investments, etc., the "cash-ability" of which may be in doubt.

Exactly the same description applies to the dual character of Liabilities. Certain debts such as current Accounts Payable and Bank Loan Payable would be placed in the upper section of the liability side of the Balance Sheet. Other Slow, or Fixed indebtedness, such as long-term Real Estate mortgage, would be placed in the lower part of the Liability side of the Balance Sheet.

It will help us if we can visualize the Balance Sheet as a "box-like" formation with each item belonging either above the imaginary Line as Current, or below the Line as Fixed or Slow.

ASSETS		LIABILITIES	
Cash	$ 5,000	Accounts Payable	$ 8,000
Accounts Receivable	10,000	Bank Loan Payable	5,000
Inventory	15,000		
Total **Current** Assets	$30,000	Total **Current** Liabilities	$13,000
Real Estate	$25,000	Real Estate Mortgage	$10,000
Trucks	5,000	Net Worth	37,000
Total Assets	$60,000	Total Liabilities	$60,000

Perhaps the most important concept of the Balance Sheet is the distinction between **Working Capital** and **Capital**. These two terms are often misunderstood and misconstrued by many businessmen, and the vital necessity of knowing the exact nature of each cannot be exaggerated.

Briefly, **Working Capital** is the net dollar difference between total **Current Assets** and total **Current Liabilities.**

1. Definition of Current Assets — those assets which, in the normal and natural course of business operations, move onward through the process of sales distribution until they become cash and become available for payment of current debts. For instance, inventory is sold on credit terms creating an Account Receivable which, when paid by the customer, becomes cash. Technically, a Current Asset is one which becomes converted into cash within, at most, one year from the date of the Balance Sheet. Actually, and realistically, a good Current Asset should result in cash within one to three months time. Accounts Receivable should be paid within 30 to 90 days and a good part of Inventory should "turn over" (be sold) at least every three months.

2. Definition of Current Liabilities — those debts which are due and payable within, at most, one year from the date of the Balance Sheet. Actually, most Current Liabilities are due and payable within a period of 30 to 90 days, such as accounts payable for inventory purchased, short term bank loan, next month's rent, etc.

Based on these definitions, Working Capital is calculated:

ASSETS		LIABILITIES	
Cash	$ 5,000	Accounts Payable	$ 8,000
Accounts Receivable ...	10,000	Bank Loan Payable	5,000
Inventory	15,000		
Total Current Assets	$30,000	Total Current Liabilities	$13,000
	$30,000	Current Assets	
	13,000	Current Liabilities	
	$17,000	= Working Capital	

Working Capital represents the amount of theoretical funds the company has on hand to conduct its business for the next 30 to 90 days. In other words, after paying all current bills and notes due, salaries, taxes, and any other accrued current liabilities, there remains $17,000 for the monthly mortgage payment, owners' drawings, dividends, (if a Corporation), plus a reserve for contingencies.

For the bank loan officer and the credit man, who hopes his extension of credit will be short term, Working Capital is the most important consideration in the Balance Sheet. Not only does the amount of Working Capital indicate whether or not there are adequate funds available to operate the business, but the size of Working Capital is a "Cushion" for unsecured short term creditors in the event of unforeseen difficulties.

The term **Capital** represents the owner's total equity in his business, including not only his equity in Current Assets (which is Working Capital), but also his equity in Fixed and Slow Assets, such as Real Estate, Trucks, etc. Again, refer back to the "box-like" formation of the Balance Sheet.

Finally, near the end of our first brief glimpse of a typical Balance Sheet, there are two Asset Subdivisions of great importance, and interestingly enough, each has a diametrically opposite meaning and value in the Financial Statement:

1. **Liquid Assets** — this term is strictly and separately the combined total of **Cash** and **Accounts Receivable** alone, which together represent the amount of dollars on hand, or to be received within the next 30 to 90 days. Using our original statement example, Cash and Accounts Receivable total $15,000 which is more than enough to pay total Current Liabilities of $13,000. In other words, if we never sold another dime's worth of inventory, we would still have enough to pay all our current debts.

Conversely, if Cash plus Accounts Receivable were $15,000, but Current Liabilities were $25,000, we would certainly be in a tight position with real cause for concern.

2. **Intangible Assets**—these are the exact opposite of valuable Liquid Assets. Intangible items are such doubtful so-called Assets as Goodwill, most Patents, Special Franchises, Leasehold Improvements (money spent to improve rented quarters), etc. This type of questionable asset whenever it appears in the statement should always be deducted from the book value of Net Worth to arrive at **Tangible Net Worth.**

The Corporation Balance Sheet

Our first sample statement would apply to either a Proprietorship or a Partnership — total Assets less total Liabilities equals Net Worth.

The only variance between the two is that Net Worth would be split up into equal shares in a Partnership:

John Smith Capital	$20,000
William Brown Capital	20,000
Total Net Worth	$40,000

The Corporation Balance Sheet differs in two important respects:

1. Corporate Net Worth is calculated simply by adding together the **Capital Stock** and **Surplus** items.

2. If the business is operating with a profit, a special current liability, found only in corporations, comes into being — "Reserve for Federal Income Tax:"

ASSETS		LIABILITIES	
Cash	$ 5,000	Accounts Payable	$ 8,000
Accounts Receivable	10,000	Bank Loan Payable	5,000
Inventory	15,000	Reserve For Federal	
		Income Tax	1,000
Current Assets	30,000	**Current Liabilities**	14,000
Real Estate	25,000	Real Estate Mortgage ..	10,000
Trucks	5,000	Capital Stock	25,000
		Surplus	11,000
Total Assets	$60,000	**Total Liabilities**	$60,000

The book value of Corporate Net Worth in any case is simply the adding together of all types of Capital Stock and all types of Surplus — in this example Net Worth equals $36,000 which is Stockholders Equity in the Company.

It will be recalled that a Proprietor and Partners must pay a Federal Income Tax, regardless of how much they may draw out for themselves, on their **entire** net profit. A Corporation pays Salaries to its Officers (usually the owners), but then the Corporation is taxed on its own residual net profit (double taxation).

Since there is nothing so certain as "Death and Taxes," a Corporation must set up a special bookkeeping Reserve Account for income taxes which are surely payable at the end of the business year. The dollar amount of this Reserve is estimated, and it varies with the indicated dollar amount of net profit being earned from month to month.

General Comments On The Balance Sheet

The first Financial Statement, the Balance Sheet, can be imagined as a still snapshot picture of the financial condition of a company at the end of any business day. After several hours of commercial activity, the books are closed at 5 P.M., and the motion of debits and credits ceases. We could then:

CURRENT ASSETS

1. Take our Cash balance in the bank from the checkbook.
2. Total up unpaid Accounts Receivable on the books.
3. Calculate an **estimated** dollar amount of inventory on hand.

CURRENT LIABILITIES

1. Total up Accounts Payable outstanding.
2. Insert the balance owing on Bank Loan.
3. Include any other debts payable within the next several months.

Here, then, is the still snapshot picture of our Current financial position. At the end of this particular day, we would hope to see reflected in the picture sufficient combined Cash and Accounts Receivable to take care of at least the majority of current debt, and adequate dollar Working Capital to take us through the next few months of operation.

But the Balance Sheet does not remain still—the next morning's incoming mail will trigger the bookkeeping motion all over again:

1. Checks from customers in payment of bills will be received. These increase Cash deposits in the bank; and decrease Total Accounts Receivable.

2. A delivery of merchandise to replenish stock will increase Inventory, and also increase Accounts Payable by a similar amount.

3. Our bookkeeper might mail out checks in payment of some of our own bills due, which decreases Cash in Bank and decreases Accounts Payable.

Thus, the Balance Sheet undergoes continuous changes, but at any time, we can total our Assets and Liabilities for a quick overall look at our financial selves. In fact, one of the many services of an Accountant is to submit periodically a "Trial Balance" which, while not exact, will indicate whether or not we are maintaining our financial equilibrium.

At about this point, a major question becomes almost audible—but how can we tell if our condition is favorable or unfavorable? Our first attempt at Analyzing Financial Statements is as follows:

FAVORABLE
(Corporation)

ASSETS		LIABILITIES	
Cash	$ 5,000	Accounts Payable	$ 15,000
Accounts Receivable ..	25,000	Bank Note Payable ...	10,000
Inventory	40,000	Federal Income Tax Payable	5,000
Current Assets	70,000	**Current Liabilities**	30,000
		Real Estate Mortgage ..	20,000
Real Estate	50,000	Capital Stock	30,000
Equipment	20,000	Surplus	60,000
Total Assets	$140,000	**Total Liabilities**	$140,000

Working Capital = $40,000
Net Worth = $90,000

Conclusions:

1. There is a substantial margin of Current Assets ($70,000) over Current Liabilities ($30,000) giving us Working Capital of $40,000, which alone would almost pay our **Total** debt of $50,000. In fact, Current Assets are more than double Current Liabilities (2.3 to 1).

2. Combined Cash and Accounts Receivable of $30,000 by themselves are sufficient to pay entire **Current Liabilties** of $30,000 (Liquidity).

3. Including the mortgage, total debt is $50,000 which is moderate in relation to corporate Net Worth of $90,000. In other words, the owner's interest in the business is almost twice as large as is the interest of creditors, a most relaxing comparison.

UNFAVORABLE

Cash	$ 1,000	Accounts Payable	$ 25,000
Accounts Receivable ..	25,000	Bank Note Payable ...	20,000
Inventory	40,000	Federal Income Tax	
		Payable	5,000
Current Assets	66,000	**Current Liabilities**	50,000
		Real Estate Mortgage	20,000
Real Estate	50,000	Capital Stock	20,000
Equipment	20,000	Surplus	46,000
Total Assets	$136,000	**Total Liabilities**	$136,000

Working Capital = $16,000
Net Worth = $66,000

Conclusions:

1. Current Assets exceed Current Liabilities by only $16,000 (Working Capital) which is completely inadequate in relation to Current Liabilities of $50,000 alone.

2. Combined Cash and Accounts Receivable of $26,000 could pay only about one-half of Current Liabilities.

3. Including the mortgage, total debt is $70,000 which is excessive in relation to corporate Net Worth of $66,000. In other words, creditors have a **greater** interest in the business than do the owners. As Total Debt continues to increase above Net Worth, in the near future the owners might decide to give up on the business.

It will be stressed in subsequent discussions that it is often impossible to make a complete and accurate analytical judgment on the basis of one Balance Sheet alone. For instance, a statement at the calendar year end of December 31, 19X9 gives us a static insight to the financial condition as of the end of the year 19X9, but, without previous year's Balance Sheets dated December 31, 19X8 and December 31, 19X7 we would be unable to study **Trends** in the business. Steady progress upwards from year to year in the dollar amounts of Working Capital and Net Worth are most encouraging. Continued declines in those same dollar amounts could point to the beginning of the end.

Finally, the Balance Sheet is probably the most important of the three financial statements, but it cannot be evaluated and interpreted accurately without the presence of the other two statements, the Profit and Loss Statement and the Reconciliation of Net Worth Statement.

QUESTIONS ON CHAPTER III:

1. What is your understanding and description of the first Financial Statement, "The Balance Sheet?"

2. Describe and define the principal Assets and then Liabilities which make up the Balance Sheet.

3. What do we mean by "the Dual Character of the Balance Sheet?"

4. Can you differentiate between "Working Capital" and "Capital, or Net Worth?"

5. Define and describe:
   a. Current Assets
   b. Current Liabilities
   c. Liquid Asset
   d. Intangible Asset
   e. Fixed Asset
   f. Long Term Liability

6. How do you calculate Net Worth in a Proprietorship, in a Partnership, and in a Corporation?

7. What are some of the factors which make for a **Favorable** Balance Sheet?

8. Name some factors which indicate an **Unfavorable** Balance Sheet.

WORKING CAPITAL CHANGES

As a Net Profit is earned, or a Net Loss suffered in the Profit and Loss Statement (P&L), the Balance Sheet is changed in several ways. A Net Profit coming into the Balance Sheet will increase Net Worth, and a Net Loss will decrease Net Worth, but Working Capital can change in several ways.

THE "DUAL CHARACTER" OF THE BALANCE SHEET

Current Asset   Current Liabilities

Working Capital
―――――――――――――――――――――――――――――――――――――――
Fixed Assets   Long Term Liabilities

Net Worth

TOTAL ASSETS EQUAL TOTAL LIABILITIES

A Net Profit coming in to increase Net Worth can go several places in the "Box Formation" of the Balance Sheet. Also, other factors can change Working Capital above the Line:

1. An **Increase** in a Current Asset (such as more Cash, or Receivables, or Inventory) will **Increase** Working Capital.

2. An **Increase** in a Fixed Asset below the Line (such as buying a new truck) will **Decrease** Working Capital above the Line.

3. A **Decrease** in a Fixed Asset below the Line (such as selling for cash an old truck) will **Increase** Working Capital above the Line.

4. A **Decrease** in Long Term Liability below the Line will **Decrease** Working Capital above the Line.

5. A Net Loss from the P & L Statement will **Decrease** Working Capital below the Line.

6. An **Increase** in a Long Term Debt below the Line (such as getting a new mortgage on Real Estate, or a Long Term Bank Loan) will **Increase** Working Capital above the Line.

7. Depreciation taken at Statement date will **Increase** Working Capital above the Line. Depreciation **Decreases** a Fixed Asset below the Line, and therefore **Increases** Working Capital above the Line. This is a good example of how Depreciation of Fixed Assets can help pay a Debt or a Loan because Depreciation does not require the use of Cash.

CHAPTER IV

THE PROFIT AND LOSS STATEMENT

The second of the three Financial Statements is a mathematical accounting formula which follows a complete and uniform pattern. Briefly, the Profit and Loss Statement is a listing of all dollar income and all dollar expense over a specified period of time with a residual net profit or loss.

Sales and expenses can be taken easily from the records and books of account, but how do we arrive at the dollar amount of our Gross Profit on the sale of merchandise? The answer is the "Cost of Goods Sold" calculation, a small formula within the Profit and Loss Statement:

Inventory at the beginning of the period —

add Purchases during the period —

Subtract Inventory at the end of the period.

Finally, subtract this remainder from Net Sales to arrive at Gross Profit.

Net Sales		**$271,151**
Cost of Goods Sold:		
Inventory, January 1, 19X8	$ 54,230	
Add Purchases for the Year	230,312	
	284,542	
Subtract Closing Inventory as of December 31, 19X8	61,743	
Cost of Good Sold		222,799
Gross Profit		**$ 48,352**

27

This traditional calculation of the "Cost of Goods Sold" must be memorized because, as we will see later, taxable net profit can be manipulated by an arbitrary increase or decrease in the dollar amount of Closing Inventory.

Here follows a Proprietorship or a Partnership report of a wholesale or retail operation for the full year from January 1, 19X8 to December 31, 19X8.

Gross Sales:		$ 272,506
Less Discounts Allowed		1,355
Net Sales		271,151
Cost of Goods Sold:		
Inventory on January 1, 19X8	$ 54,230	
Add Purchases For the Year	230,312	
	284,542	
Subtract Closing Inventory as of December 31, 19X8	61,743	
Cost of Good Sold		-222,799
Gross Profit:		48,352
Expenses:		
Employee Wages	$16,012	
Commissions to Salesmen	11,630	
Advertising	1,263	
Delivery Expense	412	
Light and Heat	603	
Telephone	180	
Insurance	1,132	
Interest on Loans	186	
Legal and Accounting Fees	600	
Bad Debts Charged Off	1,263	
Depreciation	432	
Total Expenses		$ 33,713
Net Profit:		$ 14,639

Note that a proprietor would enjoy the full net profit of $14,639, but, if there were two partners, each would be entitled to one half, or $7,319.50 apiece.

The Profit and Loss Statement of a Manufacturer

Since the manufacturer **produces** his own goods from raw materials to the finished product, there are two major differences in the calculation of The Cost of Goods Sold:

Net Sales:		$ 563,020
Cost of Goods Sold:		
Inventory on January 1, 19X8	$112,600	
Add Purchases For the Year	431,021	
Add Labor Wages	52,060	
Add Freight Expense	5,403	
	601,084	
Subtract Closing Inventory as of December 31, 19X8	140,612	
Cost of Goods Sold		-460,472
Gross Profit		$ 102,548

There are three definite stages in the manufacturing process, and **Inventory** as a whole is broken down into three parts — Raw Materials; Goods in Process of Manufacture; and Finished Goods. In other words, a manufacturer's Inventory is the combined total of Raw Material, plus Goods in Process of manufacture, plus Finished Goods.

The Corporation Profit and Loss Statement

A Proprietor and Partners pay their Income Tax based on the full net profit of the business, and the cash to make the tax payment is included in their drawings from the business.

However, the Corporate financial statement varies from the others in three important respects:

1. "Officer's Salaries" appears as an expense item.

2. Final Net Profit is further reduced by the estimated dollar amount of the Income Tax thereon. "Reserve for Income Tax" is treated as an "Expense."

3. This estimated Income Tax is carried over into the Balance Sheet among Current Liabilities as "Reserve for Income Tax."

Example:

Gross Sales:		$ 272,506
Less Discounts Allowed		1,355
Net Sales		271,151
Cost of Goods Sold:		
Inventory as of January 1, 19X8	$ 54,230	
Add Purchases For The Year	230,312	
	284,542	
Subtract Closing Inventory as		
of December 31, 19X8	61,743	
Cost of Goods Sold		-222,799
Gross Profit		48,352
Expenses:		
Officer's Salaries	$ 9,000	
Employee Wages	16,012	
Commissions	11,630	
Advertising	1,263	
Delivery Expense	412	
Light and Heat	603	
Telephone	180	
Insurance	1,132	
Interest on Loans	186	
Legal and Accounting Fees	600	
Bad Debts Charged Off	1,263	
Depreciation	432	
Total Expenses		42,713
Net Profit Before Income Tax		5,639
Reserve for Income Tax		1,880
Net Profit After Income Tax Reserve		$ 3,759

Then to the Balance Sheet:

ASSETS		LIABILITIES	
Cash	$ 8,232	Accounts Payable	$ 28,603
Accounts Receivable .	25,061	Bank Loan Payable ...	20,000
		Reserve for	
Inventory	61,743	Income Tax	3,659
Current Assets	95,036	Current Liabilities	52,262
		Real Estate Mortgage	26,000
Real Estate	55,603	Capital Stock	40,000
Trucks	5,411	Surplus	37,788
Total Assets	$156,050	**Total Liabilities**	$156,050

In this manner, the corporation wisely sets aside $1,880 and the Income Tax will be paid out of Current Assets just as any other current debt.

The Profit and Loss Statement for a Service company not engaged in the sale of merchandise would omit the "Cost of Goods Sold." Net Profit would be figured as a simple subtraction of Expenses from Sales.

Comments on the nature of "The Cost of Goods Sold" formula:

In this calculation, the mathematical fact is that the larger the **closing** inventory, the larger the net profit. Conversely, the lower the **closing** inventory, the lower the net profit. Within this neat bit of conjuring, is the average businessman's deepest personal secret — what dollar value shall I put on my year end Inventory? As a very general rule, Accountants are not asked to total up all the various items in Inventory which should be priced at **cost** or present **market** price, whichever is lower. This is the "private" area where net **taxable** profit can be manipulated — the owner takes his own inventory with the help of employees and submits a certain total dollar amount to the accountant for inclusion in the financial statement.

If it appears that the year has been a most profitable one, **closing** inventory can be arbitrarily reduced, profit then becomes lower and the Income Tax thereon becomes less objectionable.

Example of normal closing Inventory taken at **actual cost or present market value, whichever is lower:**

Net Sales		$ 271,151
Cost of Goods Sold:		
Inventory as of January 1, 19X8	$ 54,230	
Add Purchase For the Year	230,312	
	284,542	
Subtract Closing Inventory on December 31, 19X8	61,743	
Cost of Goods Sold		-222,799
Gross Profit		$ 48,352

Now in order to reduce profit, let's just cut down the dollar value of closing inventory to, say, $58,743*:

Net Sales		$ 271,151
Cost of Goods Sold:		
Inventory as of January 1,19X8	$ 54,230	
Add Purchases For The Year	230,312	
	284,542	
Subtract Closing Inventory as of December 31, 19X8	58,743*	
Cost of Goods Sold		225,799
Gross Profit		$ 45,352

Thus, by saying to ourselves that a portion of inventory has been on the shelves too long, or is obsolete, we have reduced our income tax liability.

The frustrating paradox here, and it has occurred many times, is that we may save ourselves some income tax dollars, but our financial statement is less impressive when submitted to the bank for a loan. Then the banker hears the following — "Actually, George, my inventory is priced very conservatively, and it is really worth a lot more." Nevertheless, the loan will be judged solely on the basis of figures submitted.

The third Financial Statement "Reconciliation of Net Worth," is closely aligned with Net Profit. If a Net Profit is earned, that Net Profit must equal precisely the gain, or increase in Net Worth from the preceding year end.

RECONCILIATION OF NET WORTH

The word Reconciliation is defined as "an explanation of inconsistencies," and this is precisely the function of the Third Financial Statement.

Up to this point, we have concerned ourselves with one **Balance Sheet**, and one Profit and Loss Statement dated as of the close of only one particular period of time. But it is impossible to analyze or understand thoroughly a financial condition on the basis of any single statement alone. A minimum of two years is required and preferably more in order to follow the trends, upward or downward — most particularly, the **Trend in Net Worth.**

Net Profit is transferred from the Profit and Loss Statement into the Balance Sheet as an **increase** in Net Worth, or Surplus (if a Corporation). These two balance sheet items **accumulate** net earnings over the years. Similarly, a Net **Loss** for an operating year is transferred into the Balance Sheet as a **decrease** in Net Worth, or Surplus. If Net Worth increased exactly by the dollar amount of Net Profit, or decreased exactly by the amount of Net Loss, then, clearly, the change in Net Worth from that one year to the next would need no further explanation. However, if a Net Profit were earned, and yet Net Worth **declined**, we would have to seek the reason for the decrease. We would ask for a "Reconciliation of Net Worth Statement."

Net Worth (Partnership) at close of business on
December 31,19X7: $56,840

Net Worth (Partnership) at close of business on
December 31,19X8: $50,400

Net Profit For Year Ended December 31,19X8 was $ 7,450

With a fair net profit of $7,450, Net Worth might have been expected to increase from $56,840, to $64,290, but Net Worth actually **declined** by $6,440 from $56,840 to $50,400.

Reconciliation of Net Worth

Net Worth on December 31, 19X7	$56,840
Add Net Profit for Year 19X8	7,450
	64,290
Less Partners Drawings	13,890
Net Worth on December 31, 19X8	$50,400

Now we see that the Partners drew out for themselves not only the entire net profit of $7,450, but also took out an additional $6,440 from the working capital of the business. If this trend were to continue for a few more years, these gentlemen might be out of business.

Assume we were dealing with a Corporation having Capital stock of $30,000:

Surplus on December 31, 19X7	$26,840
Add Net Profit After Income Tax	7,450
	34,290
Less Dividends Paid	13,890
Surplus on December 31, 19X8	$20,400

In this case, stockholders voted themselves excessive Dividends nowhere nearly justified by net profit of only $7,450.

To become a little more complicated:

Surplus on December 31, 19X7	$26,840
Add Net Profit After Income Tax 19X8	7,450
	34,290
Less Dividends Paid	13,890
	20,400
Less Payment to the Internal Revenue Department for settlement of prior years' disputed Income Tax Liability	3,080
Surplus on December 31, 19X8	$17,320

In other words, this company had engaged in a running battle with the Internal Revenue Service for the past two years, and finally made a cash settlement with the government. The money to clear up this matter had to be taken out of Surplus.

QUESTIONS ON CHAPTER IV:

1. Define the "Cost of Goods Sold Formula." What is the result of this Formula and what does it mean to you?

2. How, then, do we arrive at Net Profit?

3. How does the "Cost of Goods Sold Formula" differ in the case of a manufacturer?

4. Explain the difference between a Proprietorship and Partnership Profit and Loss Statement and that of a Corporation.

5. What do we mean by "double taxation" in a Corporation?

6. How can Closing Inventory at the end of the year affect final Net Taxable Profit?

7. Define the "Reconciliation of Net Worth Statement."

8. How can we tell if a business is going ahead or losing ground?

CHAPTER V

SIX IMPORTANT FINANCIAL RATIOS

Regardless of one's skill and ability to analyze Financial Statements, the calculation of the following Ratios serves three important purposes:

1. Act as a double-check, so that important features of the Statements will not be overlooked.
2. Compare with other Companies in the same line of business.
3. Reveal a satisfactory financial condition, or act as signposts of financial trouble.

1. **Current Ratio:**

   Divide Current Liabilities into Current Assets:

   Current Assets = $24,000.

   Current Liabilities = $12,000

   Current Assets exceed Current Liabilities by **2 to 1**

This 2 to 1 Ratio (or better) is the traditional, time honored Ratio which indicates a sound Current position. However, in recent years due to Inflation, Income Taxes and greatly increased Sales Volumes, Current Ratios of less than 2 to 1 (say 1.5 to 1) could be acceptable.

Actually, the Current Ratio is another way of expressing Working Capital, and the better the Current Ratio, the larger the "cushion," or safety margin, for creditors.

2. **Liquidity:**

The extent to which combined "Cash" plus "Accounts Receivable" together compare with Current Liabilities.

Cash	$10,000	Current Liabilities — $38,000
Accounts Receivable	30,000	
Total	$40,000	

$$1.05, \text{ or Liquidity Ratio is } 105\%$$

$$38,000 \overline{)40,000.00}$$
$$\underline{38,000}$$

$$2\ 000\ 00$$
$$1\ 500\ 00$$

Thus, Cash plus Accounts Receivable exceed Current Liabilities, a fine and healthy condition. Divide Current Liabilities into total of Cash and Accounts Receivable. Conversely, if the total of Cash and Accounts Receivable of $30,000 were exceeded by Current Liabilities of $50,000, the condition would be far from liquid.

This Liquidity comparison **excludes** Inventory which might be large and slow moving. But, if the condition is "Liquid," the Analyst would not worry so much about the real value of Inventory.

In the view of the writer, "Liquidity" is the most important test of the **quality** of a company's Working Capital. Working Capital could be a large dollar amount ($125,000), **but** Cash and Accounts Receivable could come no where near covering Current Liabilities. This would mean that heavy dependence would have to be placed on the value of Inventory, which might be slow moving and of questionable resale value.

3. Total Debt to Net Worth:

Divide **Tangible** Net Worth into **Total** Liabilities:

Total Debt = $50,000
Tangible Net Worth = $100,000

$$.50\%$$
$$100,000 \overline{)50,000.00}$$
$$\underline{50,000}$$

In other words, Total Debt is only 50% of Net Worth. This is a happy condition because the Owner's Equity in the business is twice that of Creditors.

Conversely, if Total Liabilities were $80,000 and Net Worth was $80,000 this Ratio would be 100%. This would mean that Creditors ($80,000) had an equal interest in the business with the owner's equity ($80,000). As Total Debt increases **above** Net Worth, Creditor's interest in the business becomes greater and greater than the owner's interest. This is the path to Bankruptcy, when Debt grows to the point where

Creditors become the larger "owners" of the business. Creditors then take over the business, liquidate the Assets, and divide what is left amongst themselves.

In almost every approaching Bankruptcy, Total Debt will substantially exceed Tangible Net Worth.

4. Average Collection Period:

This ratio is a test of the **quality** of Accounts Receivable, which must be related to Sales Volume:

Accounts Receivable multiplied
by 360 days, then
Divided by Sales

Accounts Receivable = $ 20,000
Sales   = 150,000

20,000	150,000) 720,000 (47 days
× 360	600,000
12,000.00	12,000.00
60,000	10,500.00
72,000.00	

Thus, we see that the average Account Receivable is collected within 47 days. The traditionally desirable Collection Period is 30 days, but in these days of tight money and excessive credit, 47 days is acceptable.

This Collection Period Ratio is helpful, in the absence of specific information, but an actual "aging" of Accounts Receivable is much better for an accurate analysis of Receivables:

Accounts Receivable due under 30 days — $10,000
Accounts Receivable due under 60 days — $ 8,500
Accounts Receivable past due over 90 days — $ 1,500

In this manner, we can see exactly the risk of potential Bad Debt Loss which in this case is reasonably low. This detailed information can be obtained from the company's Accounts Receivable Ledgers, or preferably can be submitted by the company's outside Accountant.

Turning to the Income and Expense Statement (Sales less Expenses yielding a Profit, or Loss):

5. Inventory Turnover

Very simply, divide Inventory into Sales.

Inventory = $ 40,000
Sales   = $160,000
               4 times

40,000)160,000
        160,000

In this case Inventory "turned over" four times in a year. Here it becomes necessary to understand the nature and peculiarities of the line of business involved. For instance, for a Retail Hardware or Lumber business, 4 times turnover in a year would be favorable. However, if you are analyzing a Wholesale Liquor Company, the turnover of inventory should be ten times per year or better, because of a large sales volume, low profit margin in that type of business.

6. Net Profit on Sales:

Divide Net Sales into Net Profit.

Sales   = $150,000
Net Profit   =   10,000
               .066 — or 6.6%

150,000)10,000.00
          9,000.00
          1,000.00

Thus, this company earned a Net Profit of 6.6% on its sales volume which would be considered favorable in any line of business.

All of these Ratios may be compared for normalcy with statistics and averages compiled by Dun & Bradstreet, Inc. covering a large number of Financial Statements in many different lines of business. This valuable comparative information is contained in the Dun & Bradstreet booklet entitled "Key Business Ratios."

In the following chapter, we begin our first analysis of an actual, live Financial Statement on a Retail Lumber Company.

QUESTIONS ON CHAPTER V:

Define and show the method of calculation of the Six Important Ratios:

1. Current Ratio

2. Liquidity

3. Debt to Worth

4. Average Collection Period of Accounts Receivable

5. Inventory Turnover

6. Net Profit on Sales

CHAPTER VI

A FAVORABLE FINANCIAL STATEMENT

This will be a necessarily long chapter as we attempt to make our first Financial Statement Analysis as complete and searching as possible. One very important suggestion — take in hand pencil and paper and make your own calculations of such items as Working Capital, Net Worth, etc. and mathematically figure out Ratios for yourself. This is the best and only way of grasping and retaining these Methods of Analysis.

S. & A. Lumber Co., Inc., Buffalo, New York
Retail Building Materials and Hardware

	Dec. 31, 19X7	Dec. 31, 19X8
Cash on hand and in Bank	$ 33,804.07	$ 23,318.53
Accounts Receivable	55,292.23	54,987.94
Inventory (Merchandise)	83,234.16	99,425.64
Prepaid Expenses	3,953.00	8,205.06
TOTAL CURRENT ASSETS	$176,283.46	$185,937.17
Building and Equipment at Cost:		
111,028.85		111,028.85
Less		
Depreciation 76,762.76		63,074.50
Net Book Value	34,266.09	47.954.35
Investment in Hardware Association	4,110.34	3,169.34
TOTAL ASSETS	$214,659.89	$237,060.86
Accounts Payable	$ 33,491.57	$ 36,101.72
Bank Note Payable in one year	6,000.00	6,000.00
Note Payable to Officer	23,019.30	28,490.82
Reserve for Income Taxes	4,403.00	6,711.50
CURRENT LIABILITIES	$ 66,913.87	$ 77,304.04

Balance of Bank Note Payable		
after one year	$ 13,500.00	$ 7,500.00
Capital Stock	50,000.00	50,000.00
Surplus	84,246.02	102,256.82
TOTAL LIABILITIES	$214,659.89	$237,060.86

Having received the Accountant's Financial Statement, we now must "spread," or condense the figures for a two year comparison, pennies excluded:

	19X7	**19X8**
Current Assets	$176,283.00	$185,937.00
Current Liabilities	66,913.00	77,304.00
Working Capital	$109,370.00	$108,633.00
Fixed or Slow Assets (below the line)	38,376.00	51,123.00
Bank Note — Portion due after one year	13,500.00	7,500.00
Net Worth (Capital Stock plus Surplus)	$134,246.00	$152,256.00

(NOTE: Net Worth Increased by $18,010 between 19X7 and 19X8.)

Now, the two year comparative "Profit and Loss Statements":

NET SALES, after discounts allowed	$546,456.95	$613,905.38
COST OF GOODS SOLD:		
Inventory 1-1-X8	$ 73,619.33	$ 83,234.16
Plus Purchases	427,875.43	478,342.23
Plus Freight In	3,892.14	5,299.18
	505,386.90	566,875.57
Less Inventory of 12-31-X8	83,234.16	99,425.64
Cost of Goods Sold	422,152.74	467,449.93
Net Sales	546,456.95	613,905,38
Subtract Cost of Goods Sold	422,152.74	467,449.93
GROSS PROFIT	$124,304.21	$146,455.45

OPERATING EXPENSES:	19X7	19X8
Salaries — Store	$ 8,080.00	$ 7,430.00
Salaries — Drivers	24,114.36	25,634.57
Trading stamps	712.50	500.00
Repairs and maintenance — Yard	111.00	133.00
Repairs and maintenance — Buildings	373.15	622.10
Repairs and maintenance — Trucks	2,204.32	1,715.33
Repairs and maintenance — Store equipment	4.83	50.03
Store Supplies	237.58	391.11
Electricity	658.41	639.96
Heat	239.13	313.35
Depreciation — Building	1,634.46	1,624.95
Depreciation — Trucks	1,031.37	1,825.08
Depreciation — Store fixtures	717.73	375.48
Depreciation — Yard equipment	229.22	301.02
Depreciation — Store equipment	25.80	25.80
Depreciation — Land improvements	476.52	425.22
Taxes — Property	2,690.06	3,543.11
Taxes — Payroll	3,303.77	2,824.97
Gas and Oil	2,929.61	2,283.63
Insurance Workmen's Compensation	1,085.00	791.82
Insurance Fire and general	3,603.09	3,273.34
Licenses and registrations	251.50	232.50
Water	32.00	32.00
Miscellaneous	104.63	48.79
TOTAL OPERATING EXPENSES	$ 54,850.04	$ 55,037.16
ADMINISTRATIVE EXPENSES:		
Officers' salaries	$ 42,311.14	$ 27,538.17
Office salaries	9,218.50	8,842.40
Travel	712.57	536.42
Office supplies	1,178.79	1,238.47
Telephone	2,389.89	2,247.90
Postage	492.20	498.13
Repairs and maintenance — Office	446.00	485.17
Depreciation — Automobiles	3,427.81	1,039.20
Depreciation — Office equipment	399.92	743.80
Advertising	6,840.91	6,118.68
Legal and professional fees	1,062.49	1,273.92
Dues and subscriptions	1,112.97	750.68
Bank charges	26.40	49.44
Life insurance — Officer	1,944.00	1,614.13
Donations	205.00	58.00
Employees' benefits	2,246.15	1,830.37
Sundry	71.00	62.25
TOTAL ADMINISTRATIVE EXPENSES	$ 74,085.74	$ 54,927.13
TOTAL OPERATING AND ADMINISTRATIVE EXPENSES	$128,935.78	$109,964.29

	19X7	19X8
OPERATING PROFIT	$ 14,339.92	$ 17,519.67
ADD OTHER INCOME:		
Discounts on Purchases	7,635.63	10,736.90
Interest Received	0	18.21
Increase in Cash Surrender		
Value of Life Insurance	1,300.00	1,300.00
	8,935.63	12,055.11
Total Operating Profit Plus		
other Income	23,275.55	29,574.78
LESS OTHER DEDUCTIONS:		
Interest Paid	1,270.95	1,904.62
Bad Debts	104.76	(105.74)
NET PROFIT BEFORE INCOME TAX	21,476.67	28,199.07
LESS INCOME TAXES	5,570.01	8,188.27
NET PROFIT FOR YEAR		
TRANSFERRED TO SURPLUS	$ 15,906.66	$ 20,010.80

So now we have seen two of the Financial Statements — the Balance Sheet and the Profit and Loss Statement. And yet, we cannot fully understand what happened between 19X7 and 19X8 without having the Third Financial Statement — "The Reconciliation of Net Worth." Go back to the Net Profit of $20,010 for the year 19X8, but note that Net Worth increased only by $18,010 after that nice profit. We need the "Reconciliation of Net Worth" statement to find the answer to this $2,000 discrepancy. Ordinarily, Net Worth should increase exactly by the full amount of Net Profit retained in the business:

Capital Stock Dec. 31, 19X7		$ 50,000
Surplus Dec. 31, 19X7		84,246
Corporate Net Worth		
Dec. 31, 19X7	=	$134,246
Add Net Profit for year 19X8	+	20,010
		$154,256
Deduct Dividends		
Declared Dec. 31, 19X8	—	2,000
Corporate Net Worth		
Dec. 31, 19X8	=	$152,256

Thus, the Third Financial Statement reveals that a modest Dividend was paid to Stockholders, and the gain in Net Worth is "Reconciled."

There is yet another Financial Statement — "Reconciliation of Working Capital," also known as "Application of Funds." Since Working Capital is most important in the daily conduct of the business, did Working Capital increase nicely during the past year, or did it decline?

Working Capital 19X7	$109,369
Working Capital 19X8	108,632
	(737)

In spite of a good net profit of $20,010 in 19X8, Working Capital actually **declined** by $737.

If we will go to the "box" concept of the Balance Sheet:

Current Assets	Current Liabilities
Working Capital	

Fixed Assets	Long Term Liabilities

Net profit coming into the Balance Sheet can increase Working Capital nicely above the Line, if that profit goes to **increase** Current Assets or to **decrease** Current Liabilities. Working Capital, however, will decline if net profit is spent on new Fixed Assets below the Line, or is used to pay off Long Term Liabilities below the Line.

Here is what happened to Working Capital in 19X8:

1. The Company purchased new trucks and equipment (Fixed Assets) during 19X8, as Fixed Assets went up from $34,266 to $47,954, an increase of $13,688 below the Line.

2. $6,000 of Net Profit was used to pay down on Long Term Debt below the Line, reducing this from $13,500 to $7,500 in 19X8.

3. "Investments" went down from $4,110 in 19X7 to $3,169 in 19X8 as the Company sold off $941 in its "Investments," which increased Cash above the Line.

4. Finally, the cash payment of a Dividend to Stockholders of $2,000 reduced Working Capital by that amount.

Reconciliation of Working Capital between 19X7 and 19X8:

	19X7	19X8
Current Assets	$176,283	$185,937
Current Liabilities	66,913	77,304
Working Capital	$109,370	$108,633

	$109,370
	108,633
(737)	Decline in Working Capital

Incoming Net Profit 19X8	$ 20,010
Less purchase of new equipment	13,688
	6,322
Less pay down on long term debt	6,000
	322
Plus cash from Sale of Investments	941
	1,263
Less payment of cash dividend	2,000
Decline in Working Capital	(737)

In summary, Net Profit retained in the business can increase Working Capital above the Line, but if that Profit is spent on items below the Line, Working Capital will decline. In the case of S. & A. Lumber Co., slightly **more** than Net Profit was used below the Line so that Working Capital declined by $737.

Statement Analysis of S. & A. Lumber Co., Inc.

Every complete Credit Folder containing Financial Statements to be appraised and analyzed should contain a copy of the latest Dun & Bradstreet Credit Report. Dun & Bradstreet, Inc. is a nation-wide mercantile financial and credit reporting Agency, and subscribers to that service can order reports on any business or company in the United States. We begin our Analysis of S. & A. Lumber Co., Inc. with a copy of the Dun & Bradstreet Credit Report:

Dun & Bradstreet — Business Information Report

November 14, 19X9	**Started**	**Rating**
S. & A. Lumber Co., Inc.	1945	C+1

280 Elm Street
Buffalo, New York
Building Materials and Hardware

John P. Shepard, Pres. and Treas.
Arthur S. Ashley, Vice Pres.
Mrs. Arthur S. Ashley, Secy.
Directors: The Officers

Summary:

Trade Payments — Generally Discount
Sales — $613,900
Net Worth — $152,200
Employs — 10
Business Record — Clear
Condition — Strong
Trend — Upward

Trade Payments:

	High Credit	**Owe**	**Past Due**	**Terms**	**Payments**	**Sold Since**
1)	$4,000	0	0	2% - 10 days	Discounts	4 Yrs.
2)	5,000	0	0	2% - 10 days	Discounts	2 Yrs.
3)	5,000	0	0	2% - 15 days	Discounts	2 Yrs.
4)	2,000	500	0	5% - 15 days	Discounts	3 Yrs.
5)	2,000	1,000	0	5% - 15 days	Discounts	4 Yrs.
6)	2,000	2,000	0	2% - 10 days	Discounts	5 Yrs.
7)	2,000	1,000	0	2% - 10 days	Discounts	1 Yr.
8)	500	500	0	1% - 10 days	Discounts	2 Yrs.

Financial:

	Dec. 31, 19X3	Dec. 31, 19X6	Dec. 31, 19X8
Current Assets	136,832	150,506	185,937
Current Liabilities	86,499	50,508	77,304
Working Capital	50,333	99,998	108,633
Net Worth	85,337	118,339	152,256

Latest Statement on File is dated Dec. 31,19X8:

Cash	25,318	Accounts Pay.	36,101
Accts. Rec.	54,987	Owe Bank 1 Yr.	6,000
Inventory	99,425	O her Current Liab.	35,201
Current Assets	179,730	Current Liab.	77,302
Net Fixed Assets	47,954	Owe Bank after 1 Yr.	7,500
Investments	2,640		
Cash Value Life Insurance	529	Capital Stock	50,000
Prepaid Expenses	8,205	Surplus	102,256
Total Assets	239,058	Total Liab.	239,058

Sales 19X8— $613,905; Gross Profit $146,455; Net Profit $20,010; Fire Insurance on contents $80,000; Fire Insurance on Building $82,000. Also extended coverage on Business Interruption. Prepared from Statement by John C. May, Certified Public Accountant, received by mail May 12, 19X9 over signature of John P. Shepard, Pres. and Treas.

Shepard said that Sales were up about 15% over 19X7. Working Capital adequate for needs with trade comment favorable. Condition regarded as strong with trend upward.

Banking:

Bank reports deposit balances in good five figures. Unsecured loans in five figures handled as agreed. Relations at bank very satisfactory.

History:

Incorporated under New York laws Feb. 9, 1949 with paid in Capital Stock of $50,000. The Corporation succeeded John P. Shepard who started this business individually in 1945.

John P. Shepard, born 1910, married, was employed by Westinghouse Electric Co. as a salesman for 5 years, and by New York Light & Power Co. for 3 years before starting this business in 1945 with $15,000 in savings plus a bank loan of $10,000. He is majority stockholder.

Arthur S. Ashley, born 1912, married, was employed by Northern Lumber Co., Buffalo, New York for several years before joining this company in 1959.

Operation:

Company retails lumber, interior woodwork, doors, sashes, frames, other building materials and hardware. Also retails line of carpeting and home decorating materials. Ten are employed.

Location:

Owns and occupies one story frame building including office and warehouse, which is attractive and well maintained, located on a commercial street.

END OF REPORT

The Dun & Bradstreet report has proven quite valuable, and has given us considerable new information:

1. The history and background of Shepard and Ashley indicate solid business experience. This business has been successfully established for almost 25 years. Their record is clear — no bankruptcies, attachments, or other business difficulties.

2. Most important, we have picked up a partial Financial Statement dated December 31, 19X8, which reveals the growth of Working Capital and Net Worth from 19X3 to 19X8.

3. We are pleased to see that company bills are paid very promptly and "Discounts" are taken uniformly. If terms of payment are "2% ten days," this means that the company may take off 2% of the total bill if payment is made within 10 days' time.

4. Also, we are assured that adequate Fire Insurance is maintained.

FINANCIAL STATEMENT ANALYSIS

	Dec. 31, 19X3	Dec. 31, 19X7	Dec. 31, 19X8
Current Assets	136,832	176,283	185,937
Current Liabilities	86,499	66,913	77,304
Working Capital	50,333	109,370	108,633
Long Term Debt	0	13,500	7,500
Fixed Assets	47,954	38,376	51,123
Net Worth	85,337	134,246	152,256
Sales	613,900	546,456	613,905
Net Profit After Taxes	Not Submitted	15,906	20,010
Dividends	0	0	2,000

Ratios:

Current Ratio	1.5 to 1	2.6 to 1	2.4 to 1
Liquidity	———	130%	101%
Debt to Net Worth	101%	60%	55%
Average Collection Period	———	36 Days	45 Days
Inventory Turnover	———	6½ times	6 times
Net Profit on Sales	———	3%	3.2%

(We urge the reader to calculate mathematically these Ratios
for himself)

History:

Successfully established for almost 25 years, with a clear business
record; management has good experience and ability. From an
original investment of $25.000, Net Worth has increased to
$152,256 at the end of 19X8 by the retention of consistent Net
Profits after Taxes and Dividends.

Financial:

Almost all the important financial categories show substantial
gains and excellent progress in the four year period under review.
It is interesting to note that Working Capital did not increase
in 19X8 in spite of a Net Profit of $20,000 for the year. The reason
for Working Capital remaining about the same as in 19X7 is: (see
previous Reconciliation of Working Capital).

Nevertheless, Working Capital of $108,600 continues quite adequate for the needs of the business. In fact, the additions to Plant and Equipment were reasonable and necessary.

The Ratios reaffirm the good progress made by the management of this good company. Current Assets exceed Current Liabilities by better than 2 to 1 at last year end. Cash plus Accounts Receivable alone cover all of Current Liabilities. Whereas in 19X3 Total Debt was slightly more than Net Worth (creditors had an investment in the business equal to the owner's equity), in 19X8 Total Debt of $84,000 was only about one-half the owner's Net Worth of $152,000. The Average Collection Period of Accounts Receivable at 45 days reflects an aggressive collection policy.

Inventory Turnover of 6 times a year is very good for the Lumber business, a further favorable comment on the purchasing judgment and ability of the management.

Net Profit of a little more than 3% on Sales seems small, but this company paid over $8,000 in State and Federal Income Taxes. This graphically points up one of the many problems and frustrations of owners of Small Businesses. Because of Taxes (and Inflation) it is almost impossible to accumulate enough Surplus over the years to conduct and operate the business on one's own Capital. Thus, there is a heavy reliance on and need for bank loans, both short term Seasonal loans and long term Capital bank loans.

Note that in 19X8 the Officers reduced their Salaries by $15,000. This sacrifice led to a better Net Profit and gain in Net Worth, increasing Capital.

Conclusion:

The writer recommends that a loan of $50,000 be granted to the subject company either (1) for a short term seasonal loan to be mostly repaid in three months, or (2) a longer term Capital loan to be paid from Net Profit plus Depreciation over a period of three years.

These loans are further reasonable because the $50,000 loan is less than ½ Working Capital of $108,000 and only 1/3 of Net Worth of $153,000.

S. B. Costales
Vice President

In the following Chapter, we will review and analyze other very Favorable Financial Statements. Following these, we will then turn to Unfavorable Statements with their tales of woe.

QUESTIONS ON CHAPTER VI:

1. Calculate for yourself the Six Important Ratios on S. & A. Lumber Co. for 19X7 and 19X8.

2. Using the two year Comparative Statements and Ratios, make your own Analysis and Conclusion on this company.

There is no necessity whatever for you to agree with the author. Look hard for errors, and come to your own conclusion.

CHAPTER VII

DEPRECIATION

There is one final segment of the Profit and Loss Statement that must be understood before any complete analysis of Financial Statements can be made. That is "Depreciation," an Expense which does **not** require the expenditure of Cash.

The Profit and Loss Statement contains many items of Expense such as salaries, rent, insurance, office supplies, etc., all of which must be paid for out of Cash. The Expense item of Depreciation, however, does **not** require the expenditure of any Cash. Depreciation is a "Bookkeeping" figure representing a write-down of Buildings, Equipment, Trucks, etc. (all Fixed Assets) from their original dollar cost. The Internal Revenue Service has set guidelines for the dollar amount the Service will allow to be taken each year. Here is where a good Tax Accountant is needed for specific details. As a general rule, a company may take Depreciation of 3% per year on the original cost of a Building, and 10% per year on Equipment and Machinery. Thus, if a Building cost $50,000, Depreciation of $1,500 could be taken as an Expense each year, for a final write-off in 33 years.

Returning to the Balance Sheet of S. & A. Lumber Co., Inc., the cost of Buildings and Equipment (Fixed Assets) was a total of $111,028.85. Over the years, a Reserve for Depreciation of $63,074.50 has accumulated, so that in the Balance Sheet you have the **Net** figure of $47,954.35, subtracting the accumulated years' Depreciation from the cost. Total Depreciation for the year 19X8 was $7,942.83 and this was added to the 19X7 Depreciation Reserve to bring the Reserve up to $63,074.50 as of December 31, 19X8. Then, in 19X9, the following year, another year of Depreciation will be added to the Reserve in the Balance Sheet, until theoretically those Fixed Assets will be written off the books completely. As a practical matter, additions and improvements are made to Buildings and new Equipment is purchased as time goes by; this increases the Cost of those Fixed Assets, which will be depreciated again from year to year. Profit and Loss Statement as an Example:

Sales	———
Cost of Goods Sold	———
Gross Profit	———
Expenses:	
Salaries	———
Rent	———
Other	———
Depreciation	$2,000
Total Expenses	
Net Profit	$4,000

Since Depreciation as an Expense does not require the expenditure of Cash, Depreciation actually becomes part and parcel of Net Profit. In our later analyses, we will add Depreciation to Net Profit. As in this example of $4,000 Net Profit plus Depreciation of $2,000 reveals that the company earned a complete profit of $6,000.

Finally, since cash was **not** reduced by the Expense of Depreciation, there must be an adjustment in the Balance Sheet so that Assets will balance with Liabilities. The adjustment is that the "Reserve for Depreciation" is increased by the amount of Depreciation taken for the past fiscal year in the P & L.

The principal point to remember here is, simply, that Depreciation must be added to Net Profit in any analysis of the total "profitability" of a company.

As we Analyze Financial Statements in the following Chapters and attempt to justify Bank Loans to these companies, we will see the importance of "Depreciation."

Basically, there are only three types of Commercial Bank Loans:

1. Seasonal, self-liquidating Loans. For Instance, a Retail Department Store in October must purchase extra merchandise for the upcoming Christmas Season. A $20,000 bank loan is taken in October to pay for this Seasonal Inventory increase. Most of the merchandise is sold in December, creating Cash and Accounts Receivable. These Accounts Receivable are collected mostly in January and February and the Bank Loan

is paid off or reduced substantially. This is the classic "Seasonal" loan, which has little to do with Net Profit earned by the business. The Bank Loan is paid by the purchase and sale (liquidation) of Inventory, and we call it a "Short Term Loan." This type of bank loan is further classified as a "Short Term Working Capital Loan." All the action is above the Line. Fixed Assets and Long Term Liabilities are not involved in the "Short Term Working Capital Loan."

Assume that the management of S. & A. Lumber Co., Inc. borrows $50,000 from its bank for a three month period to purchase Merchandise Inventory for the upcoming Spring and Summer season. Inventory increases by $50,000 and as the merchandise is sold Cash and Accounts Receivable build up by the dollar amount of those sales. Then as customers pay their bills to S. & A., Accounts Receivable go down and Cash increases to pay off the "Short Term Working Capital Loan" within a three month period.

2. Bank Loans for the purchase or improvement of Buildings, Machinery, new Trucks or Equipment (Fixed Assets) **cannot** be paid in the same manner as a self-liquidating Working Capital Loan. A loan for the purchase of Fixed Assets can only be repaid from Net Profit. We would propose that a "Term Loan" be arranged for a period of three years with principal payments plus interest every three months.

3. The "Capital" Loan. During the past many years of Inflation and heavy Income Taxes on Small Businesses, it has become more and more difficult for an owner of a Small Business to retain profits which might increase his Net Worth or Capital. Each year, it takes more dollars of Capital to support a growing sales volume to purchase inventory, give pay raises and benefits to employees — Inflation has added greatly to the

cost of doing business. Then, when a good profit is realized at the end of the year, Income Taxes (and other Taxes) siphon off 35% to 40% of those profits which otherwise might have been kept in the business to increase Capital.

Consequently, the small businessman has become more and more reliant on **bank loans** to supplement his own "Capital." Now, certainly, these "Capital" Loans cannot be repaid in 3 or 4 months. These "Capital" Loans are used as Working Capital in the daily conduct of the business because the management has not been able to accumulate and retain enough of its own Capital. Repayment of this type of loan must come from Net Profits after Taxes, plus Depreciation and must be repaid on a long term basis. Assume a $50,000 "Capital" Term Loan is taken to bolster the owner's Capital, and Net Profit after Taxes plus Depreciation is $20,000 per year, or better. Then the company could repay the bank "Capital" loan at the rate of $16,600 per year over a period of three years.

It has been interesting to note over the years, the increasing number of so-called short term, 90 day bank loans which are renewed for another 90 days time after time. Many of these "Short Term" loans would continue, with modest reductions, for several years. There comes a time when the bank and the Small Businessman must recognize the nature of the "Capital" loan, and must reschedule the loan for regular quarterly repayments of principal over a period of from 3 to 5 years, depending on the amount of Net Profit plus Depreciation.

Here again, the dollar amount of yearly "Depreciation" is most important. Assume that Net Profit per year is only $15,000, but "Depreciation" is $5,000 per year. Since "Depreciation" does not require the expenditure of Cash, that $5,000 can be added to Net Profit of $15,000 to repay the "Capital" Loan. When calculating the repayment of any long term loan, always add "Depreciation" to Net Profit.

Depreciation is always welcomed as an "Expense" because it reduces Taxable Net Profit.

QUESTIONS ON CHAPTER VII:

1. Give your understanding of "Depreciation," both in the yearly P & L Statement and its effect on Fixed Assets in the Balance Sheet.

2. In arriving at true Net Profit available to pay off a loan, why is "Depreciation" so important?

3. Describe and discuss:

   a. A Short Term Working Capital Bank Loan

   b. A Long Term Equipment Loan

   c. A Long Term Capital Loan

CHAPTER VIII

FAVORABLE FINANCIAL STATEMENTS

Acmo TV and Appliance Co.

140 Main St., Springfield, Mass.

ASSETS	Dec. 31, 19X4	Dec. 31, 19X7	Dec. 31, 19X8
Cash	$ 12,395	$ 14,245	$ 18,053
Accounts Receivable	14,859	32,705	45,008
Inventory	11,370	30,017	26,143
Current Assets	38,624	76,967	89,204
Prepaid Expenses	0	1,064	1,064
Store Building & Equipment After Depreciation	13,720	30,534	27,549
Total Assets	$ 52,345	$108,566	$117,817
LIABILITIES:			
Notes Payable	$ 0	$ 4,209	$ 0
Accounts Payable	15,253	46,945	45,850
Accrued Taxes	1,683	4,124	4,124
Real Estate Mortgage Short Term Portion	1,303	313	0
Current Liabilities	18,239	55,591	49,974
Proprietor Net Worth	34,106	52,975	67,843
Total Liabilities	$ 52,345	$108,566	$117,817
Net Sales	$142,511	$376,472	$438,767
Gross Profit	34,241	51,309	57,474
Operating Expenses	21,663	13,270	15,956
Net Profit	12,578	36,998	41,518
Current Assets	38,624	76,967	89,204
Current Liabilities	18,239	55,591	49,974
Working Capital	$ 20,385	$ 21,376	$ 39,230
Net Worth	$ 34,106	$ 52,975	$ 67,843

Calculate the Six Important Ratios for each year.

PROFIT & LOSS STATEMENT

DECEMBER 31, 19X4

Gross Sales		$143,479.04
Less Discounts	$ 147.40	
Less Returns	820.04	967.44
Net Sales		142,511.60
Beginning Inventory	8,599.63	
Purchases	89,894.59	
Labor	19,373.24	
Total	117,867.46	
Less Ending Inventory	9,596.87	
Cost of Goods Sold		108,270.59
Gross Profit		$ 34,241.01
Less Operating Expenses:		
Supplies, Trans. on Purchases,		
Selling Expense	$ 5,350.30	
Lights, Phone, Fuel, Misc.		
Expense, Accounting	2,523.64	
Advertising, Truck, Dues &		
Subscriptions, Repairs,		
Interest Expense	5,380.57	
Taxes	5,367.96	
Bad Debts	628.71	
Depreciation	2,411.02	
Total Operating Expenses		21,662.20
NET PROFIT		$ 12,578.81

STATEMENT OF EARNINGS

JANUARY 1 TO DECEMBER 31, 19X7

Net Sales		$376,472.69
Cost of Goods Sold:		
Inventory, January 1, 19X7	$ 12,116.75	
Purchases	280,226.44	
Freight	1,434.54	
	293,777.73	
Inventory, Dec. 31, 19X7	—30,017.11	
Cost of Goods Sold	263,760.62	
Expenses:		
Service Labor Cost	39,617.39	
Depreciation	6,074.85	
Taxes	3,199.54	
Heat and Lights	1,968.94	
Maintenance of Trucks	3,781.49	
Insurance	6,760.47	
		325,163.30
		$ 51,309.39
General and Administrative Expense:		
Office Salary	3,200.00	
Telephone	976.73	
Stationery and Postage	833.91	
Legal and Auditing	1,025.00	
Cleaning	625.45	
Rent	2,535.10	
		9,196.19
		$ 42,113.20
Selling Expense:		
Advertising	3,959.98	
Commission	115.00	
		$4,074.98
		$ 38,038.22

Deductions:

Interest	746.44	
Miscellaneous	271.17	
Dues	24.00	
		1,041.61
Earnings, 19X7		$ 36,996.61

STATEMENT OF EARNINGS

JANUARY 1 TO DECEMBER 31, 19X8

Sales - Net		$438,767.22
Cost of Goods Sold:		
Inventory, January 1, 19X8	$ 30,017.11	
Purchases	288,872.51	
Freight	1,414.27	
	320,303.89	
Inventory, Dec. 31, 19X8	— 26,143.19	
Cost of Goods Sold	294,160.70	
Expenses:		
Service Labor Cost	55,053.88	
Depreciation	6,595.97	
Taxes	16,259.82	
Heat and Lights	2,065.31	
Maintenance of Trucks	4,966.26	
Insurance	1,485.79	
Refunds	705.26	
		381,292.99
		$57,474.23

General and Administrative Expense:

Office Salary	5,131.53	
Telephone	1,178.45	
Stationery and Postage	1,722.76	
Legal and Auditing	1,532.75	
Cleaning	1,592.55	
Rent	2,247.60	
	————	
		13,405.64
		————
		44,068.59

Selling Expense:

Advertising	1,953.14	
Commission	10.00	
	————	
		1,963.14
		————
		42,105.45

Other Deductions:

Interest	80.98	
Miscellaneous	502.30	
Dues	5.00	
	————	
		588.28
		————
Net Earnings, 19X8		$41,517.17
		————

	19X4	19X7	19X8
Current Ratio	2 to 1	1.4 to 1	1.8 to 1
Liquidity	150%	116%	126%
Debt to Worth	52%	103%	73%
Average Collection Period	37 days	30 days	30 days
Inventory Turnover	13 times	12 times	16 times
Net Profit on Sales	8%	9.8%	9.3%

These comparisons are very interesting because the Ratios themselves tell the whole story of this business in the three year period under review.

Observe the very substantial increases in Sales volume from $142,500 in 19X4 to $438,700 in 19X8. Ordinarily, one would expect to see good sized bank loans to support larger Inventory and Accounts Receivable as the result of very much larger Sales. Not so in this case — there were no bank loans at all as of December 31, 19X8. The owner (proprietor) of Acme TV and Appliance Co. very smartly used his good credit standing with his wholesale suppliers to carry sufficient Inventory in his store **without** paying interest on bank loans. Note that Accounts Payable were greater than Inventory in 19X7 and 19X8.

In spite of this moderate strain on the Owner's Capital (Net Worth), the Ratios all ended up favorably in 19X8:

1. Current Ratio almost 2 to 1.
2. Liquidity was excellent, as Cash plus Accounts Receivable of $63,000 were 26% greater than Current Liabilities of $49,900.
3. Total Debt of $49,900 was considerably less than the Owner's Net Worth of $67,800. The Owner's Capital (Net Worth) exceeded creditors interest in the business by 27%, a happy situation.
4. The Average Collection Period of Accounts Receivable was very good at 30 days. Fast incoming cash from customers allowed the Owner to pay his wholesale suppliers promptly.
5. Inventory turned over 16 times in the year 19X8, a remarkably fast turnover of merchandise. Here is another reason why bank loans were not necessary.
6. Net Profit on Sales at 9.3% showed a fine return on sales volume. This, of course, increased the Owner's Net Worth (Capital) which helped to finance the increased amount of business.

Reconciliation of Net Worth:

Net Worth 19X8	$67,843
Net Worth 19X7	52,975
Net Worth Gained only	14,868 during the year,

although Net Profit was	41,518

Net Worth Dec. 31, 19X7	52,975
Add Net Profit for 19X8	41,518
	94,493
Less Owner's Drawings (Salary)	26,650
Net Worth, Dec. 31, 19X8	$67,843

Reconciliation of Working Capital:

Working Capital, 19X8	$39,230
Working Capital, 19X7	21,376
Working Capital Gain	$17,854

Incoming Factors:

Net Profit	$41,518
Decrease in Fixed Assets	2,985
Total Incoming	$44,503

Outgoing Factor:

Drawings (Salary)	26,650
Net Gain in Working Capital	$17,853

As we have seen previously, an Increase in Fixed Assets (below the Line) will cause a **Decrease** in Working Capital. Conversely, a Decrease in Fixed Assets will cause an **Increase** in Working Capital as above. As far as Working Capital (above the Line) is concerned, an **Increase** in Fixed Assets is an "Outgoing Factor," and a **Decrease** in Fixed Assets is an "Incoming Factor."

Conclusion:

All the important financial categories showed excellent gains and progress during the three years under review. Working Capital almost doubled, as did Net Worth. Sales and Net Profit were up remarkably.

The Owner is to be congratulated on his fine managerial performance as a Small Businessman.

A third "Favorable" Financial Statement:

The City Water Company, Inc.
Bristol, Virginia

	Dec. 31, 19X6	Dec. 31, 19X7	Dec. 31, 19X8
Cash	$ 19,142	$ 20,494	$ 21,099
Accounts Receivable	4,367	4,783	8,555
Inventory	7,655	7,961	6,904
Prepaid Expenses	811	735	811
Current Assets	31,975	33,975	37,370
Plant & Equipment — after Depreciation	381,037	385,303	394,818
Office Equipment	5,823	4,563	5,656
Total Assets	$418,835	$423,842	$437,845
Accounts Payable	$ 8,753	$ 3,740	$ 1,717
Accrued Expense	2,069	6,578	6,523
Reserve Income Tax	3,203	5,015	4,903
Current Liabilities	14,025	15,333	13,143
State & Town Grants in Construction	91,155	91,859	97,120
Accrued Expenses	3,017	2,784	7,423
Long Term Mortgage on Real Estate	94,000	92,000	90,000
Preferred Stock	20,000	20,000	20,000
Common Stock	105,000	105,000	105,000
Earned Surplus	91,987	96,865	105,157
Total Liabilities	$418,835	$423,842	$437,845
Working Capital	$ 17,950	$ 18,640	$ 24,227
Net Worth	216,987	221,865	230,157
Sales	108,884	112,068	112,969
Expenses	98,632	93,686	94,488
Net Profit — After taxes	10,252	18,382	18,481
Depreciation	14,273	14,601	14,694

Net Profit plus depreciation	$ 24,525	$ 32,983	$ 33,175
Less Dividends	9,150	9,150	9,150
Available for debt retirement —	$ 15,375	$ 23,833	$ 24,025

Here we have a Public Utility Company furnishing water to people and industry in the small town of Bristol, Virginia.

One of the items in the Balance Sheet needs explanation, and is peculiar to Public Utility companies. "State and Town Grants in Construction" represents money granted and given by Towns and the State to the Utility, and no repayment is required. The "Liability" is in the Balance Sheet only for bookkeeping purposes, and it can be disregarded as a Debt. In order to encourage and help Utilities to expand their Water Supply and Service to more and more homes as they are built, the State and Towns make these grants, or gifts.

Another item for comment is "Preferred Stock," in addition to "Common Stock," as part of the Capital structure. In general, Preferred Stockholders have certain privileges and preferences over Common Stockholders, possibly as to the payment of Dividends before Common Stockholders, or a "first" or preferred position of repayment in the event of liquidation of the corporation. These conditions and stipulations vary, and one must read the terms of each Preferred Stock Indenture in each specific case.

Ratios:

	19X6	19X7	19X8
Current Ratio	2.2 to 1	2.2 to 1	2.7 to 1
Liquidity	160%	170%	223%
Debt to Worth	45%	42%	42%
Average Collection Period	13 days	13 days	23 days
Net Profit on Sales	9%	16%	16%

Once again, the Ratios help us to interpret and to understand the condition and the **Trend** of a business organization.

For this three year period, the overall financial condition has been excellent. Current Assets were consistently more than double Current Liabilities. Cash and Accounts Receivable were always substantially in excess of Current Liabilities. Actual Debt was only about 40% of Net Worth — in other words, creditors had only a moderate investment, or interest in the corporation.

Water bills were collected very promptly, in less than 30 days.

Net Profit of 16% on Sales after Taxes is unusually high. Public Utility companies are regulated and controlled by State Government Public Utility Commissions in all of our States. The Commission, generally speaking, tries to hold Net Profit to about 9% of Income. Thus, we can see that The City Water Co., Inc. will be asked by the Commission to reduce its charges to customers for water. This is always an unpleasant occasion for any profit-making organization, and you can be sure that there will be much talk and long bargaining between the Commissioner and the Company management.

These Financial Statements were submitted to The First National Bank of Bristol, Virginia with a request for a loan of $90,000 to purchase a nearby neighboring Water Company, The North Virginia Water Company.

Here again we have a "Capital Loan" situation, the repayment of which must be predicated and calculated on Net Profits plus Depreciation each year after Taxes and Dividends.

Referring back to our three year spread of Financial Statements, we observe that in 19X8 there was $24,000 in one year available to pay off on a Capital Loan. Now we must bear in mind that this good profit may be reduced in the future by a Public Utility Commission ruling to reduce rates charged customers which would reduce Net Profit. Therefore, we would recommend to the Loan Committee of The First National Bank of Bristol: A Term Bank loan of $90,000 to be repaid at the rate of $15,000 plus interest per year for a pay-out period of 6 years. This pay back schedule allows leeway for possible lower profits.

Note that the mortgage on company Real Estate has been declining by $2,000 every year, which is its long term amortization repayment. Therefore, we must add that $2,000 payment per year to the $15,000 payment required on the new loan under discussion. Nevertheless, Net Profits appear quite adequate for this total debt retirement.

All the Ratios are favorable, the trends are upward, and the $90,000 loan is only 40% of corporate Net Worth of $230,000.

Now we have analyzed three **Favorable** Financial Statements. In the following Chapter, we turn to **Unfavorable** Statements of Small Business which vividly reveal lack of Capital, Poor Management, and Faulty Judgment.

QUESTION ON CHAPTER VIII:

1. Calculate Ratios and make your Analysis based on the financial information submitted, both for Acme TV & Appliance Co. and The City Water Co.

CHAPTER IX

UNFAVORABLE FINANCIAL STATEMENTS

Again, we repeat — the reader must work out and calculate the "spread" of important items and the Ratios.

Auto Tire and Recapping Co.
40 Lake St., Bridgeport, Conn.

	Dec. 31, 19X6	Dec. 31, 19X7	Dec. 31, 19X8
Cash	$ 1,474	$ 4,067	$ 747
Accounts Receivable	51,338	54,977	67,236
Inventory	60,191	56,144	62,085
Current Assets	113,003	115,188	130,068
Building and Equipment			
Net after Depreciation	56,091	61,464	55,365
Investments	31,852	11,135	14,244
Prepaid Expenses	4,815	7,114	8,081
Total Assets	$205,761	$194,901	$207,758
Accounts Payable	$ 65,575	$ 83,242	$ 87,926
Note Payable Bank	9,463	13,198	23,889
Twelve Months Portion			
on Long Term Note	26,595	27,700	24,776
Accrued Taxes	9,447	12,744	20,247
Current Liabilities	111,080	136,884	156,838
Long Term Note			
Payable after 1 year	53,161	39,990	28,334
Owner's Net Worth	41,520		
Capital Stock	—	10,000	10,000
Surplus	—	8,027	12,586
Total Liabilities	$205,761	$194,901	$207,758

During 19X7, this business was changed from a Proprietorship (Sole Owner) to a Corporation. This will be discussed later on.

PROFIT AND LOSS STATEMENT
DECEMBER 31, 19X6

Sales		$316,221.33
Cost of Goods Sold:		
Inventory, beginning of year	$ 52,006.26	
Purchases	181,067.50	
Freight In	1,460.45	
Total	234,534.21	
Inventory, end of year	60,190.84	
Cost of Materials Sold	174,343.37	
Operating Expenses	69,467.03	
Total Cost of Goods Sold		243,810.40
Gross Income from Operations		72,410.93
Selling and General Expenses,		41,760.88
Net Operating Profit		30,650.05
Other Income:		
Miscellaneous	48.74	
Carrying Charges	1,042.88	
Discounts Earned	283.51	1,375.13
Total		$ 32,025.18
Other Deductions:		
Interest paid and miscellaneous	$ 6,485.75	
Bad Debts	3,557.19	
Discounts allowed	2,610.34	$ 12,653.28
Net Profit Transferred to		
Proprietor's Capital Account		19,371.90
Capital Account:		
Owner's Investment, beginning of year		36,304.42
Total Capital		55,676.32
Deduct:		
Owner's Drawings	11,546.56	
Federal Income and Self Employment Tax	2,609.40	14,155.96
Owner's Investment, End of Year		$ 41,520.36

PROFIT AND LOSS STATEMENT
DECEMBER 31, 19X7

Sales		$311,354.95
Cost of Goods Sold:		
Inventory, beginning of year	$ 59,376.25	
Purchases	178,117.76	
Freight-in	916.63	
Total	238,410.64	
Inventory, end of year	56,144.06	
Cost of Materials Sold	182,266.58	
Operating Expenses,	62,572.38	
Total Cost of Goods Sold		244,838.96
Gross Income from Operations		66,515.99
Selling and General Expenses,		48,838.91
Net Operating Income		$ 17,677.08
Other Income:		
Increase in cash value life insurance	$ 120.00	
Miscellaneous	763.59	$ 883.59
Total		18,560.67
Other Deductions:		
Discounts allowed	2,026.26	
Interest paid	5,824.29	
Bad Debts	168.22	8,018.77
Net Income Before Federal and State Taxes on Income		10,541.90
Federal and State Taxes on Income:		
Federal normal	2,528.72	
Less investment credit	832.11	
	1,696.61	
State Excise	817.49	2,514.10
Net Income Transferred to Retained Earnings		$ 8,027.80

PROFIT AND LOSS STATEMENT
DECEMBER 31, 19X8

Sales		$435,655.15
Cost of Goods Sold:		
Inventory, beginning of year	$ 56,144.06	
Purchases	266,794.45	
Freight-In	740.28	
Total	323,678.79	
Inventory, end of year	62,084.91	
Cost of Materials Sold	261,593.88	
Operating Expenses,	91,483.41	
Total Cost of Goods Sold		353,077.29
Gross Income from Operations		82,577.86
Selling and General Expenses		66,872.41
Net Operating Income		$ 15,705.45
Other Income:		
Increase in cash value life insurance	$ 1,140.00	
Miscellaneous	759.01	$ 1,899.01
Total		17,604.46
Other Deductions:		
Discounts allowed	3,044.93	
Interest paid	6,727.69	
Bad Debts	656.78	10,429.40
Net Income Before Federal and State Taxes on Income		7,175.06
Federal and State Taxes on Income:		
Federal normal	2,045.96	
Less investment credit	84.61	
	1,961.35	
State Excise	655.78	2,617.13
Net Income Transferred to Retained Earnings		$ 4,557.93

DUN & BRADSTREET BUSINESS INFORMATION REPORT

Dun & Bradstreet, Inc.
September 12, 19X8
Wholesale & Retail Tires & Recapping
Auto Tire and Recapping Co., Inc.
40 Lake St., Bridgeport, Conn.

George Goldfarb, Pres.
Mrs. G. Goldfarb, Vice Pres.
Alan Goldfarb, Secretary

SUMMARY

Payments—Slow	Employees—12
Sales—$300,000	Record—Clear
Net Worth—$20,000	Condition—Unbalanced

Trend—Downward

Payments:	High Credit	Owes	Past Due	Sold Since	Payments
	9,500	8,500	6,000	1962	Slow 90 days
	6,000	5,000	3,000	1960	Slow 120 days
	4,000	2,000	2,000	1963	Slow 90 days
	500	0	0	1967	Slow-Collected by Attorney

Financial: On Sept. 3, 19X8, George Goldfarb, Pres., declined all information when interviewed. Outside sources report debt is heavy, financial condition unbalanced, and working capital limited.

Banking: Bank reports small balances and checks sometimes returned for insufficient funds. Bank loans secured by Savings Bank Book.

History: George Goldfarb, born 1914, married, was variously employed in the tire business as a mechanic and salesman until starting this business in 1951 with small capital as a Proprietorship. On April 4, 19X7, the business was incorporated with paid in Capital Stock of $10,000. Mrs. Goldfarb appears as Vice-President, and their son, Alan, is Secretary.

Operation: Wholesales (75%) and retails (25%) tires, maintaining own capping equipment. Wholesale accounts number about 100 consisting of garages, service stations, and companies which have several cars and trucks. Owns a one-story brick building located on a main highway on outskirts of town.

END OF REPORT

Now, the "spread" of important items:

	19X6	19X7	19X8
Current Assets	$113,003	$115,188	$130,068
Current Liabilities	111,080	136,884	156,838
Working Capital	$ 1,923	($ 21,696)	($ 26,770)

(Brackets indicate red figure Deficits)

	19X6	19X7	19X8
Net Worth	$ 44,520	$ 18,027	$ 22,586
Sales	316,221	311,355 (9 months)	435,655
Net Profit	19,371	8,027	4,557
Owner's Salary	14,156	18,000	20,800

Ratios:

	19X6	19X7	19X8
Current Ratio	1.01 to 1	(Deficit)	(Deficit)
Liquidity	46%	42%	47%
Debt to Worth	400%	970%	840%
Average Collection Period	58 days	52 days	60 days
Inventory Turnover	5 times	5.6 times	7 times
Net Profit on Sales	6%	2.5%	1%

Based on the foregoing Accountant's facts, one wonders in amazement how this company can avoid Bankruptcy. Creditors, with a total investment of $185,000 in this company, are simply hanging on for dear life, hoping that the owner's well-to-do family will come to his rescue. This is highly improbable, and unlikely.

The Current Ratio is a red Deficit. Current Liabilities exceed Current Assets by $26,700, resulting in very slow and unsatisfactory payment of bills. The Accountant's Audit revealed that $21,000 of Accounts Payable were 90 days or more past due.

Liquidity is very poor. Current Liabilities exceed Cash and Accounts Receivable by 53%.

Debt is fantastically larger than the Net Worth. Debt was over eight times Net Worth in 19X8.

The collection of Receivables is slow at 60 days.

Inventory turned over satisfactorily at 7 times, but at a pathetic Net Profit.

The downward trend in Net Worth speaks volumes, and reveals possible dishonesty in the character of the Owner. His Net Worth in 19X6 was $44,500, but this declined to only $18,000 after incorporation in 19X7. Note that "Investments" went down from $31,000 in 19X6 to $11,000 in 19X7 after the corporation was formed. In order to protect himself (and maybe to defraud creditors), the Owner literally took for himself $20,000 in "Investments" from the business. Bad as it was before incorporating, the new Corporation started off in even worse shape.

Observe the increases in the Owner's Salary from $14,000 to $20,000 in 19X8.

Question:

In view of the high danger and risk in this situation, why did the bank loan more money from $9,400 in 19X6 to $23,000 in 19X8 ?

Answer:

The Owner was forced to give the bank his wife's Savings Bank Book as collateral.

Here is another case of manipulation of finances:

Smith Laundry, Inc.
125 Cross St., Northampton, Mass.

	Dec. 31, 19X6	Dec. 31, 19X7	Dec. 31, 19X8
Cash	$ 1,690	$ 2,810	$ 1,773
Accounts Receivable	6,275	6,100	5,000
Inventory	3,900	2,000	1,600
Current Assets	**11,865**	10,910	8,373

Prepaid Expenses		1,706		1,200	1,200

Machinery & Equipment at Cost	95,716		106,381		110,674	
Accumulated Depreciation	71,153	24,563	76,674	29,707	83,705	26,969

Total Assets	$38,124	$41,817	$36,542

Accounts Payable	$ 9,319	$ 7,444	$ 6,593
Bank Notes Payable	13,201	15,996	7,800
Accrued Expenses and Taxes	2,462	2,821	3,543
Loan from Robert Smith	—	5,745	4,214
Current Liabilities	24,982	32,006	22,150
Notes Payable after 12 Months	6,802	1,560	2,000
Capital Stock	5,000	5,000	5,000
Surplus	1,340	3,251	7,392
Total Liabilities	$38,124	$41,817	$36,542

For your convenience, we will condense the Profit and Loss Statements:

Sales	$136,984	$146,669	$151,777
Expenses	137,026	144,825	147,633
Net Profit	(42. Loss)	1,844	4,144
Current Assets	11,865	10,910	8,373
Current Liabilities	24,982	32,006	22,150
Working Capital-Deficits	(13,118)	(21,096)	(13,778)
Net Worth	$ 6,340	$ 8,251	$ 12,392

The outside Accountant's comments in submitting these Statements are all—important. He wrote, "The figures were taken from Books kept by the management without our Audit or confirmation. Because Accounts Receivable were estimated in round figures, as was Inventory, we cannot testify as to the accuracy of the Statements as a whole." Nor could any Analyst exactly reconcile Working Capital changes or Net Worth increases. So, in addition to a badly unbalanced Financial Condition, there is doubt about the correctness of the figures themselves.

We would not expect a strong Working Capital position in a Laundry business where there is very little Inventory, and the principal investment is in Machinery and Equipment below the Line. However, the Working Capital Deficits (Current Liabilities greater than Current Assets) in the Smith Laundry are larger than we would expect.

We will spare you the Ratios in this case, because they are all very poor. Suffice it to say that Total Debt of $24,150 is double Net Worth of $12,390.

SMITH LAUNDRY, INC.

History:

In business here for about 20 years, starting with very small capital of $5,000. After 20 years of operations, Capital and Surplus is only $12,000.

Management estimates a sales volume of over $216,000 in 19X9, $151,700 actual in19X8. It is difficult to understand how this increased sales volume can be accomplished on comparatively tiny capital funds.

Whereas, the corporation has been financially weak for years (corporate debt of $24,000 is double net worth of $12,000), Kenneth Smith and Robert Smith seem to have done rather well personally. Kenneth's net worth seems exaggerated, but he does have some securities and real estate. Robert has substantial equity in his home, in addition to a profitable Laundromat in his own name, which earned about $7,000 after taxes last year. I asked Bob if he would consider increasing his home mortgage and put the proceeds in the corporation. His answer was a quick and definite "No."

Recently, the "Mercury Cleaners" was purchased for dry cleaning and rug cleaning. Then Kenneth purchased an adjoining small lot and small house for $35,000 with the help of at least two mortgages. The intrinsic value of this property may be less than ½ the purchase price, and this speculative price is based on the proximity of relocated Route 6.

The present loan request is for $100,000 to pay out loans of $68,000 from another bank and give the corporation $32,000 in new money to extend the plant, and to purchase some used machinery. Proposed collateral would be the continuation of several real estate mortgages and chattle mortgages on laundry machinery. The real value of the 3 family house next door, and the recent speculative property purchase next to Mercury appears doubtful to the writer. The laundry machinery is many years old (**depreciation** totals **$83,000**), it is special purpose equipment, and could not be considered as anywhere near adequate collateral.

The Smith Laundry has been put on notice that it must run pipe lines to the city sewer system by the end of 19X9, and cease discharging waste into the river behind the plant. Kenneth & Bob were vague on the cost of this, but agreed it would be "a few" thousand dollars. They will have to be some kind of financial magicians to comply with this City Order.

Conclusion:

In the view of the writer, extension of any bank credit to the Smith family is out of the question. In fact, it is doubtful whether the Smith family is able to pay their present outstanding debts.

The writer could not, in good conscience, present this as an application to The Small Business Administration. Second mortgages would be required on all properties, even if The Small Business Administration should become interested.

It is now—right now—that the Smith family should realize that they must put a good deal of their own personal resources into their corporation. They should also realize that their banks have been very good to them with very substantial loans, partially secured and unsecured.

The Smiths' financial future should be in their own hands from now on.

S. B. Costales

Here we will look at Financial Statements on a different line of business—selling Real Estate and Insurance. This is also an example of Analyzing a Financial Statement even though we do not have the benefit of consecutive yearly Statements.

The Williams Agency

84 Eastern Ave., Stamford, Conn.

	Dec. 31, 19X6	Dec. 31, 19X8
Cash in Checking Account	$ 789	$ 326
Cash in Savings Accounts	17,785	10,861
Insurance Premiums Receivable	8,792	8,367
Current Assets	27,366	19,554
Real Estate for Sale at Market Value	91,579	93,595
Total Assets	$118,945	$113,149
Payable to Insurance Companies	$ 13,521	$ 18,668
Accrued Expenses and Taxes	1,556	869
Bank Note Payable	2,909	1,839
Current Liabilities	17,986	21,376
Mortgages on Real Estate	33,214	29,597
Owner's Net Worth	67,745	62,176
Total Liabilities	$118,945	$113,149
Sales	$114,448	$144,101
Expenses	98,805	133,697
Net Profit	15,643	10,404
Owner's Salary	17,973	11,527
Working Capital	9,380	(1,822)
Net Worth	$ 67,745	$ 62,176

	Dec. 31, 19X6	Dec. 31, 19X8
Current Ratio	1.5 to 1	(Deficit)
Liquidity	152%	72%
Debt to Worth	75%	80%
Average Collection Period	27 Days	20 Days
Net Profit on Sales	13%	7%

Even though we do not have the 19X7 Statement, we certainly do **not** like what we see between 19X6 and 19X8:

1. Working Capital of $9,380 in 19X6 has completely disappeared in 1968 when Current Liabilities became larger than Current Assets. Also, Liquidity has disintegrated. We must assume that Williams had a poor year in 19X7, or that he drew a substantial amount out of the business in 19X7.

2. Total Debt was 80% of Net Worth. Real Estate was put in the Balance Sheet at "Market Value," which is simply Mr. Williams guess of the price at which he hopes to sell the Real Estate. As we know, the dollar value of the Real Estate should have been put in the Balance Sheet at "Cost." Furthermore, Net Worth of $62,176 is completely represented by his Equity of $63,998 in Real Estate which probably is over-valued.

3. It could be argued that, in this case, Real Estate is much like "Inventory." If so, Real Estate "Turned Over" only 1.5 times in 19X8 (dividing Real Estate into Sales).

4. Mr. Williams' personal salary exceeded Net Profit in both years.

5. Net Worth declined by $5,569 in two years.

Turning to the Insurance selling part of this business, we find a most unfavorable condition of unbalance in 19X8:

Insurance Premiums Receivable —	8,367
Payable to Insurance Companies —	18,668
	(10,301)

In other words, Mr. Williams' customers owe him $8,367 for Insurance Policies they have purchased, **but** Mr. Williams owes his Insurance Companies $18,668 or more than **twice** what is due him. In this unhappy situation, Williams had the nerve to ask his bank for an unsecured loan of $10,000 to pay off his Insurance Company Accounts Payable.

Now our attention is focused on the nice $10,861 in Savings Banks. Mr. Williams probably figures he is pretty smart, because he is using his Credit (other people's money), and preserving his own Savings for personal, selfish security. But, somehow or other, he has gotten himself into quite a financial mess. The bank rejects the Unsecured loan, but will loan him $10,000 if he puts up his Savings Bank Books for Collateral.

Williams paid little attention to his own Financial Statement. Or, more probably, he did not have a **knowledge** of Financial Statements and would not listen to the advice of his Accountant.

QUESTIONS ON CHAPTER IX:

1. Calculate the unfavorable Ratios of Auto Tire and Recapping Co., and write your own Analysis.

2. Name and describe all the unfavorable factors.

3. How and why has this business lasted as long as it has?

4. Can you make any suggestions for rectifying this situation?

5. Similarly, comment on Smith Laundry Co. and also on The Williams Agency.

CHAPTER X

AN ACTUAL CASE HISTORY: FRAUD

Following World War II in the late 1940's, the Commercial Banks throughout the country were loaded with Depositors' cash money. There had started a change-over from the production of war materials to consumer goods (autos, electrical appliances, etc.), but this transition was not immediate. With this vast reservoir of loanable funds, the banks were eager to make loans with which they could start earning good profits once again. Consequently, certain unusual types of loans were accepted and considered proper by Bank Loan Executives, such as large loans secured by the pledge of Inventory as Collateral (Factors' Liens on Inventory).

Another new bank loaning method was to make substantial loans secured by the Assignment to the bank of Accounts Receivables. In the event of Bankruptcy, presumably the bank would be a "Preferred" creditor over other creditors, and could collect the Accounts Receivable for itself to pay off the loan.

Now, there are **two** distinctly different methods of Assignment of Accounts Receivable to a Bank or a Finance Company:

1. Assignment with **"Notification."** The procedure is for the bank customer to bring to the bank several "Invoices" or Billings rendered to the businessman's customers on account of merchandise purchased by his customers. These Invoices are Assigned over to the bank as collateral. Usually, these Billings (Invoices) are supposed to be paid within 30 days, but often payments are not received until 60 days after date of the Invoice. In the meantime the businessman bank customer needs cash, Working Capital to meet the daily needs of his business, such as Payroll, Rent, Accounts Payable, etc.

   Bear in mind that most companies would qualify for an Unsecured Working Capital loan, based solely on their good, and favorable Financial Statements. The pledging of Accounts Receivable as Collateral for a loan, however, means that we are loaning to a rather weak, or "Marginal," company. Its Financial Statements **cannot** justify an **U**nsecured bank loan. We must realize immediately that we are dealing with a company which is under financial pressure.

A Typical Invoice (or Account Receivable):

From: Northern Electric Co.
64 Main Street
Boston, Mass.

Date: Sept. 8, 19XX

To: Ed's Appliance Shop
101 Commerce Ave.
Boston, Mass.

Invoice #67543A

For:		
8 G. E. Electric Toasters		$64.11
3 Rolls copper wire		40.12
5 Telecron Electric Clocks		50.17
4 Acme Electric Dishwashers		392.25
12 Emerson Table Radios		120.82
2 Excello Color TVs		890.62
	Total Amount Due	$1,558.09

Terms: 2% discount if paid within 10 days from date. Total amount due in 30 days from date.

"This Invoice #67543A has been assigned to the Second National Bank of Boston on September 11, 19X9."

Northern Electric Company has brought this and several other Invoices totalling $20,671.09 to the bank as collateral for a loan of $16,500 (bank would loan only 80% of Total Invoices).

Notification: The Second National bank will write a letter to Ed's Appliance Shop actually notifying Ed that his account has been pledged to the bank as Collateral. The bank will verify and confirm the correctness of the Amount Due, and whether or not the Merchandise was satisfactory to Ed. The bank will also request that when Ed is ready to pay the Invoice that his check be sent directly to "Loan Department, the Second National Bank of Boston." At the bottom of this letter to Ed there will appear "The above terms and conditions outlined in this letter are hereby accepted without qualification."

Signed:

> Edward J.Moran
> Ed's Appliance Shop
> 101 Commerce Ave., Boston, Mass.
> Sept. 12, 19X9

Whereas **"Notification"** is the safer method of making an "Accounts Receivable Loan," it is still risky. For instance, Ed may find out later on that the Merchandise was not satisfactory, and he refuses to pay the Invoice. Or Ed gets in financial trouble and cannot pay.

An objection to "Notification" is often that the bank customer (Northern Electric Co.) is embarrassed to have his customers know that their Account has been pledged to the bank in order to get a loan. So Northern Electric Co. pleads for financing on a **"Non-Notification"** basis. If the bank relents and agrees to Non-Notification, the risk of loss becomes much greater.

Non-Notification: The mechanics here are the same as in the Notification loan, except that the bank does not verify the Invoice and does **not** write a letter asking for payment directly to the bank. The bank relies on the honesty and good intentions of its customer (Northern Electric Co.) to send dutifully in to the bank all checks in payment of its Accounts Receivable Invoices. The real danger here is that the bank is loaning an under-par company which has daily financial pressures. So Northern receives a check in full payment of an Invoice which should be immediately turned over to the bank to reduce the loan. However, the pressure is on Northern. One of its creditors threatens Suit unless a bill is paid. Northern uses the check it should have given to the bank to relieve this danger. Northern hopes to send the bank another check payment tomorrow, and so forth, getting deeper and deeper in trouble.

Another danger in Non- Notification is the authenticity of the Receivable Invoices themselves. And so it was that a large Northeastern Commercial Bank became involved in a $300,000 bad Loan

Loss and an eventual Bankruptcy.

We submit Financial Statements given to the bank one year preceding Bankruptcy:

K. & L. Wholesale Meat Co., Inc.

46 Union St., Newark, N.J.

	Dec. 31, 19X7	July 5, 19X7	Oct. 2, 19X7
Cash in Bank	10,322	8,212	6,002
Accounts Receivable	308,412	359,606	390,820
Inventory	260,520	240,600	250,610
Current Assets	579,254	608,418	647,430
Equipment & Trucks Net after Depreciation	40,301	45,103	51,610
Investment in Egg Market Futures	20,000	25,000	30,000
Total Assets	639,555	678,521	729,040
Accounts Payable	206,812	200,160	212,640
Bank Note—Secured by Accounts Receivable	210,607	261,800	315,162
Accrued Expenses & Taxes	10,502	12,811	15,900
Current Liabilities	427,921	474,771	543,702
Capital Stock	70,000	70,000	70,000
Surplus	141,634	133,750	115,338
Total Liabilities	639,555	678,521	729,040

	Full Year 19X7	6 Mos. 19X8	9 Mos. 19X8
Net Sales	3,207,928	1,960,211	2,980,012
Expenses	3,175,168	1,945,831	2,956,498
Net Profit	32,760	14,380	23,514
Officers' Salaries	70,600	38,400	54,000

Ratios as of Oct. 2,19X8:

Current Ratio	1.2 to 1
Debt to Worth	300%
Liquidity	72%
Average Collection Period	35 Days
Inventory Turnover	11 times
Net Profit on Sales	8/10th of 1%

We certainly can see why The K. & L. Wholesale Meat Co. did not qualify for unsecured bank credit. The only favorable Ratio was "Turnover of Inventory" at 11 times. The worst Ratio was that Debt was **three** times Net Worth. Also, note the Investment in "Egg Futures" which is pure gambling on the future price of eggs — you could win or you could lose.

Finally, the Bank Loan Committee committed an unforgivable sin by accepting Financial Statements on very odd, inconsistent dates, such as July 5 and October 2. The Bank should have insisted on regular year end plus quarterly Statements every three months (March 30, June 30, September 30, and year end December 31) prepared by an outside, independent Accountant.

It will seem almost unbelievable to you that the Loan Committee would approve loans of $300,000 even on the questionable basis of the Assignment of Accounts Receivable. The only light that can be shed on this strange loan decision is that it was said that The K. & L. Wholesale Meat Co. was "the most profitable account in the bank."

On the surface, all seemed to be going well until one day there was a rumor that K. & L. Co. was borrowing $25,000 here and there "on the side" at exorbitant interest rates from wealthy individuals. Next K. & L. started to write large checks against "Insufficient Funds" with nowhere near enough on deposit to cover these large checks. At this point, the Loan Officer became gravely concerned.

The large, six figure amount of Accounts Receivable accepted by the bank as Collateral was on the Non-Notification basis. It was alleged that these Receivables were due to the K. & L. Company from a large chain of Super Markets known as Grand National Stores, Inc. In other words, Grand National supposedly had purchased large quantities of meat from the K. & L. Company, creating large Accounts Receivable due to K. & L. Company, and which would in due course be paid to K. & L. Then K. & L. should turn these payments over to the bank to reduce the loan.

Seeing signs of real trouble, the Loan Officer belatedly telephoned Grand National to ascertain just how much Grand National owed to the K. & L. Company. To his complete shock and dismay, he was told by the Bookkeeper at Grand National — "we don't buy much from K. & L., only when we run short of certain items — let's see, Grand National as of today owes K. & L. $21,642.60."

The bank was holding in its Collateral File $380,000 of false, ficticious Account Receivable Invoices. Under heavy financial pressure from all sides, K. & L. would type up false, non-existing Invoices and bring them to the bank for "Collateral" loans.

Then high powered and high priced Lawyers were called in, and the bank took over the operations of K. & L. However, after a few months, the bank was unable to satisfy other Creditors, and K. & L. filed a Petition in Bankruptcy with heavy losses to all Creditors. Including Attorney's fees and other costs, the bank must have lost well over $300,000.

After the Bankruptcy, this wholesale meat business immediately started up again under the ownership of close relatives of K. & L. and had little difficulty getting substantial credit from meat packing houses and another bank.

QUESTIONS ON CHAPTER X:

1. Outline the difference between Assignment of Accounts Receivable on a **Notification** basis, and **Non-Notification** basis.

2. What are the hazards of each?

3. Make your own Analysis of K. & L. Wholesale Meat Co.

4. How could this large Bankruptcy have been averted?

CHAPTER XI

A FINAL UNFAVORABLE FINANCIAL STATEMENT

The following is a dramatic example of Excessive Debt, plus the abortive attempt of the Corporation Stockholders to selfishly protect themselves financially.

In March 19XX, a group of entrepreneurs purchased the Outdoor Sports Manufacturing Company of New Britain, Connecticut. As part of the purchase price, their new Corporation became indebted to the former Owners in the amount of $250,000 repayable for a period of 10 years at the rate of $25,000 per year plus interest. These heavy annual repayments could be made only from Net Profits after Taxes—if good Net Profits were earned consistently—a dubious start toward a tragic ending.

In the following condensed yearly financial comparisons, note that original Capital Stock remains steadily inadequate at $11,000. Then, in the last Financial Statement, note that the Stockholders and Officers increased their loans to their Corporation from $44,000 to $119,800—an increase of $75,800 cash.

After this maneuver, Stockholders and Officers believed that they had accomplished for their own personal benefit the following:

1. If their Corporation became profitable, then repayment of their loans from the Corporation would not be an IRS Income tax matter for them—this would be considered simply as a "Repayment of Loans."

2. If their Corporation failed and went into Bankruptcy, then Officers and Stockholders would appear as Creditors of their own Corporation, and they personally would share in whatever residual payments, however small, were made in the Bankruptcy Settlement to General Creditors.

The problem arose when the Officers requested a so-called Short-Term loan from their Bank. In view of the tiny Capital Stock and the large Stockholders' loans, the Bank required first that the Stockholders sign a legal "Subordination Agreement." The Owners would have to agree not to receive from, or demand of, their Corporation any repayments on account of loans to their Corporation until after the Bank loan is paid in full.

This proposed "Subordination" upset the Owners' best-laid plans for their own protection. They refused to sign any Subordination and their loan request was rejected by the Bank, which simply added to their Corporation's many financial problems.

The Outdoor Sports Manufacturing Company

	Dec. 31, 19X2	Dec. 31, 19X5	Dec. 31, 19X8
Cash & Accts. Rec.	$ 62,852	$ 70,621	$171,404
Inventory	66,088	91,636	146,844
Current Assets	132,001	159,523	326,260
Current Liabilities	96,697	109,863	226,933
Working Capital	35,304	49,660	99,327*
Capital Stock	11,000	11,000	11,000
Stockholders' Loans	44,000	44,000	119,800
Sales	229,547	221,871	293,875
Net Profit or Loss	(8,693)	(27,541)	7,308
	Loss	Loss	Net Profit

*This Working Capital amount was very briefly increased by the infusion of Stockholders' loans.

The above condensed three year comparisons were taken from the CPA Financial Statements. Very properly, the CPA states, "The Financial Position of the Corporation was not audited by me, and therefore I cannot express an opinion as to the accuracy of these Financial Statements as a whole."

As you can see, Ratios are badly out of Balance, Operating Losses have more than wiped out Corporate Net Worth, and the inevitable end is near.

In October 19XX, The Outdoor Sports Manufacturing Company filed a Petition in Bankruptcy.

CHAPTER XII

TRUE VALUE OF CERTAIN ASSETS

Ordinarily, Liabilities are quite definite and factual. Accounts Payable, Bank Notes Payable, Real Estate Mortgages Payable are matters of record on the books of a company, and these can be verified and confirmed.

However, the honest and real value of some Assets can be subject to question and doubt.

Luckily, the Ratios provide us with a "quality test" such as the Average Collection Period of Accounts Receivable (hopefully near 30 days). An active Turnover of Inventory is another favorable Ratio test.

But, when we go below the Line to Fixed Assets of Real Estate and Machinery and Equipment, the value and efficiency of those Assets must be scrutinized carefully. The cost figures of the Balance Sheet may show Buildings and Machinery at original cost of $56,812, less Depreciation of $12,601 for a Net Book Value of $44,211. The only way to judge and appraise the real value of those Fixed Assets is for one to go personally to the Company Plant and visually inspect those Fixed Assets. You may not be an accredited Real Estate Appraiser or an experienced Appraiser of technical machinery, but a Plant Visitation will give you an insight into the condition and efficiency of Buildings and Machinery.

As an example, some years ago, the writer visited the plant of the Horton Manufacturing Co. of Torrington, Connecticut. That old company had been in business for over 100 years manufacturing a variety of metal products. Most of the machinery, such as Lathes, Milling Machines, and Metal Turning Machinery, was reasonably modern, but still in use by the company were three antique Milling Machines driven by leather belts. The manufacturer's names of these machines were obliterated by time and grease, but, after considerable scraping and rubbing, we saw that the year 1910 was barely legible on one of the machines. Depreciation had written off the value of these machines many, many years ago. But the question, the doubt here is "inefficiency" — How could Horton hope profitably to manufacture metal products in competition with other companies, and continue to use some long out-moded and out-dated machinery? This visit to the Horton plant raised doubt about the Ability or Capacity of its Management.

Another more recent "Plant Visitation" was a revealing, eye-opening experience. The Following Balance Sheet was presented for an additional bank loan consideration:

AUDIO VISUAL ADVERTISING CO., INC.

Westfield, Mass.

March 31, 19X9

ASSETS		LIABILITIES	
Cash	$ 13,282	Accounts Payable	$ 27,080
Accounts Receivable	18,690	Bank Note Payable	45,000
Work in Process	43,893	Other Loans Payable	9,137
		Taxes Payable	4,313
		Current Portion Mortgage	4,381
Current Assets	75,865	Current Liabilities	89,911
Machinery & Fixtures	37,322	Bank Note Payable	
Motion Picture		After 1 year	23,556
Equipment	84,964	Real Estate Mortgage	43,810
Film Materials	13,329	Common Stock	7,000
Land & Buildings	75,632	Surplus	122,835
Total Assets	**$287,112**	**Total Liabilities**	**$287,112**

Although this Financial Statement is badly out of balance, actually this business is a very interesting one. The company produces film strips for visual education in schools and colleges.

However, our concentration at the moment is on the **Quality,** the **Goodness** of the Fixed Assets.

We were conducted on a tour of the Building and Plant. Directly in the middle of the building, we were surprised to observe a large fireplace over which there was a large sign saying "Boston and Albany Railroad." After some questioning, we learned that the basic part of this building was originally the local Railroad Station house which was built back in 1910. From time to time, the Audio Visual Co. had added on a room here and a room there, so that the present building is a hodge-podge, labyrinthine structure.

Note that Land and Buildings are listed in the Balance Sheet as being worth $75,632. Having viewed and inspected this Real Estate, we judged that it would be difficult to sell this property at any price, no matter how small.

What value can we put on used Motion Picture Equipment? In the unfortunate event of Liquidation of this company, who would buy this Equipment and what price?

Without a "Plant Visitation," we might have assumed that the Fixed Assets were valuable and readily saleable.

Calculate "Working Capital" and we will see that Current Liabilities exceed Current Assets by $14,046, a red deficit figure. Cash, plus Accounts Receivable of $31,972, versus Current Liabilities of $89,911 = a complete absence of "Liquidity." Total Debt was $157,277 compared to the owner's Net Worth of $129,835, for a Debt to Worth Ratio of 120%. However, after our low appraisal of the Real Estate, Net Worth would be considerably less than $129,835.

This business was started with paltry, completely inadequate Capital Stock of only $7,000. Net Profits have been earned from year to year, and creditors and the bank were intrigued (and deluded) by this glamorous, new type of advertising business. In addition, the management was obviously quite persuasive.

Whereas, we see Surplus (retained profits) of $122,835, all of this has gone into the purchase or construction of Fixed Assets of doubtful value. Therefore, heavy reliance has been placed on the willingness of creditors and the bank to support an increasing sales volume.

Finally, the bank rejected the request for additional loans, and the Loan Officer began to have grave misgivings about his present loans already on the books.

Intangible Assets:

Good Will	Franchise Cost
Leasehold Improvements	Deposit on Rent
Patents	Organization Expense

These are some of the types of Intangible Assets, which, in the event of liquidation or failure of a business, have no real value and probably could not be sold for cash. Therefore, the analyst should deduct the dollar amount of Intangible Assets from Net Worth to arrive at the true **Tangible** Net Worth.

Example

ASSETS		LIABILITIES	
Cash	$ 345.72	Accounts Payable	$ 3,821,.01
Accounts Receivable	3,072.63	Bank Note Payable	6,000.00
Inventory	6,843.17	Accrued Expense	862.50
Current Assets	10,261.52	Current Liabilities	10,683.51
Fixtures and Equipment	2,732.50	Capital Stock	10,000.00
Leasehold Improvements	682.12	Surplus Deficit	(4,352.57)
Franchise Cost	2,000.00	Net Worth	5,647.43
Organization Expense	654.80		
Total Assets	$16,330.94	**Total Liabilities**	$16,330.94

Capital Stock	$10,000.00
Less Surplus Deficit	— 4,352.57
Book Value Net Worth	5,647.43
Less Intangible Assets	
682.12	
2,000.00	
654.80	
3,336.92	— 3,336.92
Tangible Net Worth	$ 2,310.51

98

This is an unfortunate Small Business situation wherein the Owner paid $2,000 for a Franchise to sell radio parts and electronic equipment. His first ten months of operations resulted in a Loss of $4,352.57, reducing his original Capital (Net Worth) to $5,647.43. After deducting the Intangible Assets, Tangible Net Worth becomes a pathetic $2,310.51.

Once again, the irresistible urge "to go into business for myself and be my own boss" has led this Small Businessman to the brink of Failure.

QUESTIONS ON CHAPTER XII

1. How do the Ratios test the Quality of Current Assets?

2. What must you do to appraise the Quality of **Fixed** Assets?

3. After a Favorable Analysis, we would hope that a business would be successful. . . Why, then, is a realistic appraisal of the true value of Fixed Assets so important?

4. List six Intangible Assets.

5. Why does this type of Asset have little or no real value?

6. How do Intangible Assets affect Book Value of Net Worth?

CHAPTER XIII

CERTAIN SPECIAL FINANCIAL STATEMENTS

So far, we have concentrated on **Favorable** Financial Statements and then on **Unfavorable** Financial Statements. With a knowledge of Analysis and Ratios, it should be rather easy to differentiate between the Good and the Bad.

There is, however, a much more interesting and certainly more challenging type of Financial Statement. And that is a Statement on a new, or young Small Business trying to get started or struggling to expand and grow on its own inadequate starting Capital. It is in the **beginning** that a Small Business needs financial assistance the most, but it is also in the beginning when that Small Business will find it most difficult (if not impossible) to obtain financial help.

There are the time-honored three "C's" of Credit — **Character, Capacity,** and **Capital.** In the following chapters on "Financial Statements of Small Business," each real life example possessed "Character" (Honesty and Determination), and also "Capacity" (Experience and sharp business Ability) — but each lacked adequate starting **Capital** in the beginning.

The following Chapters will show that it is possible (and profitable) to help finance Small Business at a time when that assistance and encouragement is most needed.

Almost anyone can grant a Good Loan or grant Credit to an established company in good financial condition. And almost anyone can refuse a Loan, or Credit, to a company in poor financial condition. But the greatest challenge and satisfaction can be realized if we **combine** Financial Statement Analysis with a sympathetic appraisal of the human being, the individual, the person who stands behind the cold figures of his Financial Statement. Is he Honest, hard-working, and able to take disappointments and reversals without giving up? Has he had, in the past, good, sound, hard Experience in his line of business? Is there a continuing Demand for his merchandise or products? Would you vouch for his business Ability to operate the business at a profit?

If the answer is "Yes" to all these questions, and the Financial Statements presented are reasonably in balance and reasonably satisfactory, then one can, on the basis of a calculated risk, give financial aid and credit to "Certain Small Businesses." This and the next Chapters are true stories of such success.

Finally, and most important, Statement Analysts and Credit Men are all too often **negative** in their approach to and appraisal of Financial Statements. Concentration and emphasis is often put on the unfavorable aspects of the situation. Certainly, in the case of Jack Adams, (Financial Statement to follow), the loan of $36,000 was way out of proportion to his meager capital contribution of only $4,000.

Bear in mind that there are almost always **unfavorable** aspects and features in every business situation which is in need of credit and financial assistance. One can almost always find something to criticize. The trick is to put all the facts on the Balance Scale of Judgment, and then decide if the Favorable factors outweigh the Unfavorable factors. This is the **Positive** approach to any appraisal.

In the small city of Putnam, Connecticut, Jack Adams had been employed in the Gilbert Department Store on Main Street for 14 years. At first, he was only a clerk, but later on old Mr. Gilbert gave Jack more and more responsibilities, such as buying merchandise on his own, opening charge accounts, suggesting prices on merchandise, etc. In fact, the relationship between Jack and the "old man" became almost like father and son. There came the day when Mr. Gilbert, approaching 70 years of age, could no longer withstand the rigors and the stress and strain of the daily operation of his retail department store.

The natural sequence of events would be for Jack Adams to purchase this business which he knew so well. However, the selling price was $40,000, and Jack had only hard-earned Savings of $4,000. In his search for a comparatively large, long term bank loan of $36,000, he was turned down by two banks. However, a third bank Loan Officer could see the "naturalness" and the prospect of further success if Jack could become the owner of this profitable store. After much negotiating, on January 2, 19X5 The Small Business Administration agreed to loan Jack $21,000 and the bank approved the remainder of $15,000 to be repaid in monthly installments of $300, plus interest. Jack Adams had all the ingredients of success except Capital. Now he had his Capital.

After three and one-half years of operations under Jack Adams' management and direction, we present an Analysis of:

THE GILBERT DEPARTMENT STORE, INC.

82 Main St., Putnam, Conn.

BALANCE SHEET AT JUNE 30, 19X7

ASSETS

Current Assets:

Cash on hand	$ 400.00	
Cash on deposit	18,381.30	
Accounts receivable	6,077.09	
Loans and exchanges	4,130.75	
Merchandise inventory	48,496.00	
Prepaid insurance	328.94	
Prepaid organization expenses	438.40	
Total Current Assets		$78,252.48

Capital Assets:

Furniture, fixtures, etc.	7,950.56	
Automobile	4,610.64	
Improvements to leased property	4,715.74	
	17,276.94	
Less, accumulated depreciation	4,181.71	
Total Capital Assets		13,095.23
TOTAL ASSETS		$91,347.71

103

LIABILITIES AND CAPITAL

Current Liabilities:

Accounts payable, trade	$14,957.53	
Accrued accounts payable	1,618.75	
Accrued current year federal income taxes	2,060.09	
Employee payroll deduction reserves, etc.	1,515.18	
Notes payable to Bank within 12 months	3,000.00	
Notes payable on auto	621.25	$23,772.80

Total Current Liabilities

Long term debt — payable after 12 months to S.B.A. & Bank   26,372.07

TOTAL LIABILITIES   50,144.87

Capital:

Common capital stock — issued & outstanding	30,000.00	
Retained earnings	11,202.84	

TOTAL CAPITAL   41,202.84

TOTAL LIABILITIES AND CAPITAL $91,347.71

EXHIBIT B

PROFIT AND LOSS STATEMENT

FOR THE FISCAL YEAR ENDED JUNE 30, 19X7

Sales $223,962.83

Deduct,

Cost of Sales:

Inventory at June 30, 19X6	$ 52,228.54
Add, Purchases	149,411.23

Freight and express	1,541.81	
	203,181.58	
Less, Inventory at June 30, 19X7	48,496.00	
Cost of Sales		154,685.58
Gross Profit on Sales		69,277.25

Deduct,

Expenses:

Advertising	4,049.11	
Auto expenses	228.99	
Officers' salaries	18,200.00	
Labor	14,487.02	
Rent	6,375.00	
Repairs to premises	240.15	
Heat and lights	2,076.30	
Telephone	439.93	
Insurance	1,556.80	
Office expense	160.97	
Audit and legal	650.00	
Paper, boxes, twine, etc.	810.29	
Sundry expenses	1,345.83	
Taxes	3,325.97	
Contributions	24.00	
Depreciation — store fixtures and auto	3,340.21	
Alterations to clothing	43.47	
Interest paid	1,856.10	
Amortization of organization expense	109.60	
Total Expenses		59,319.74
		9,957.51
Add,		
Purchase discounts taken		3,305.32
Net Profit For The Year		13,262.83
Deduct,		
Current Year federal income taxes		2,060.09
Net Income For The Year		$ 11,202.74

THE GILBERT DEPARTMENT STORE, INC.

82 Main St., Putnam, Conn.

BALANCE SHEET AT JUNE 30, 19X8

ASSETS

Current Assets:

Cash on hand	$ 500.00	
Cash on deposit	24,188.40	
Accounts receivable	5,976.67	
Merchandise Inventory	58,816.59	
Prepaid insurance	373.94	
Prepaid organization expenses	328.80	
Total Current Assets		$ 90,134.40

Capital Assets:

	Cost	Accumulated Depreciation 6-30-68	Net Book Value
Furniture, fixtures, etc.	$ 8,791.39	$3,039.31	$ 5,752.08
Automobile	2,065.64	504.93	1,560.71
Improvements - leased property	4,997.26	2,100.89	2,896.37
	$15,854.29	$5,645.13	$10,209.16
Total Capital Assets — Net			10,209.16
Loan Due from Stockholders			12,373.17
TOTAL ASSETS			$112,766.73

LIABILITIES

Current Liabilities:

Accounts payable, trade	$ 26,278.12
Accrued Expenses	1,979.89
Accrued current year federal income taxes	2,501.35
Employee payroll deductions reserves, etc.	1,847.20

Notes payable to Bank (payable within twelve months)	3,222.88	
Notes payable to Bank on Automobile (payable within twelve months)	2,087.52	
Total Current Liabilities		$ 37,916.96
Long term debt - payable after twelve months S.B.A. and Bank	23,983.33	
Total Long Term Debt		23,983.33
TOTAL LIABILITIES		$ 61,900.29

STOCKHOLDERS' EQUITY

Common capital stock - issued and outstanding	30,000.00	
Retained earnings	20,866.44	
TOTAL STOCKHOLDERS' EQUITY		50,866.44
TOTAL LIABILITIES AND STOCKHOLDERS' EQUITY		$112,766.73

THE GILBERT DEPARTMENT STORE, INC.

82 Main St., Putnam, Conn.

PROFIT AND LOSS STATEMENT

FOR THE FISCAL YEAR ENDED JUNE 30, 19X8

Sales		$231,195.06
Deduct, **Cost of Sales:**		
Inventory at June 30, 19X7	$ 48,496.00	
Add, Purchases	168,321.01	
Freight and express	1,675.36	
	218,492.37	

Less, Inventory at June 30, 19X8	58,816.59	
Cost of Sales		159,675.78
Gross Profit on Sales		71,519.28

Deduct,
Expenses:

Advertising	5,176.76	
Auto expenses	372.56	
Officers' salaries	18,940.00	
Labor	17,099.18	
Rent	6,000.00	
Repairs to premises	195.32	
Heat and lights	1,902.75	
Telephone	433.69	
Insurance	2,094.90	
Office expense	392.96	
Audit and legal	615.00	
Paper, boxes, twine, etc.	594.59	
Sundry expenses	1,396.43	
Taxes - payroll	1,369.06	
Taxes - other	1,856.56	
Contributions	63.00	
Depreciation	2,397.28	
Alterations to clothing	8.00	
Interest paid	1,821.41	
Amortization of organization expenses	109.60	
Total Expenses		62,839.05
		8,680.23

Add,
Purchase discounts taken, etc. | | 3,484.82 |

Net Profit For The Year		12,165.05
Deduct, Provision for current year federal income taxes		2,501.35
Net Income For The Year		$ 9,663.70

THE GILBERT DEPARTMENT STORE, INC.

	19X7	19X8
Current Assets	$ 78,252	$ 90,184
Current Liabilities	23,772	37,916
Working Capital	54,480	52,268
Fixed Assets & Other Assets Net	13,095	22,582
Total Assets	91,347	112,766
Long Term Debt	26,372	23,113
Capital Stock	30,000	30,000
Surplus	11,202	20,866
Net Worth	$ 41,202	$ 50,866
Sales	$233,962	$231,195
Net Profit	11,202	9,663
Net Worth Gain	17,376	9,664
Owner's Salary	18,200	18,940
Current Ratio	3.3 to 1	2.4 to 1
Liquidity	104%	80%
Average Collection Period	9 Days	9 Days
Inventory Turnover	4.6 times	3.9 times
Debt to Net Worth	120%	120%
Net Profit on Sales After Taxes	4.8%	4.3%

Comments on the Statements for 19X7 - 19X8

1. Notes Payable to Small Business Administration and Bank—that portion due within the next 12 months is a **Current** Liability (Refer to definition of a Current Liability) above the "Line." The remainder is below the "Line" as a Long Term Liability.

2. Improvements to Leased Property (store building) is an "Intangible" Asset, and should be deducted from Net Worth. Money was spent to improve the store building which was owned by someone else.

3. In 1968, "Loan due from Stockholders" (asset) represented money borrowed from the Corporation by Stockholders (Jack Adams and his wife) to be used as a down payment on the purchase price of the store building here. This property will soon be owned jointly by Mr. and Mrs. Adams and they will lease it back to the Corporation.

4. Sales in 19X5 were $166,425 and this has increased to $231,195 in 19X8 under the management of Jack Adams.

5. In 19X5, Jack's salary was $10,000, but in 19X8 he was able to pay himself almost $19,000.

Net Worth is easily Reconciled because Net Worth Gain equals Net Profit coming into the Balance Sheet.

RECONCILIATION OF WORKING CAPITAL

Working Capital 19X7		$54,480
Working Capital 19X8		52,268
Working Capital Decrease		$ 2,212
From Working Capital:		
Fixed & Slow Assets Increased		$ 9,487
Paydown on Long Term Debt		2,389
		$11,876
Into Working Capital:		
Net Profit 19X8		9,664
Working Capital Decrease		$ 2,212

In other words, "Slow" Assets below the Line increased about equal to Net Profit coming into the Balance Sheet. Jack Adams has negotiated to buy the store building and has taken as a loan the down payment ($12,373) for this purchase out of his Corporation's Working Capital. Ordinarily this might raise a few eyebrows, but in this case the business is profitable, Net Worth is increasing year by year, and Working Capital should recover and increase in the next year. Why spend money on a building owned by someone else? The purchase of the store building was proper judgment.

The only really unfavorable Ratio (120%) is that Total Debt is 20% more than the owner's Net Worth — in 19X8 Total Debt was $61,000 versus Net Worth of $50,000. The reason for this disproportion is obviously the S.B.A. and bank loan taken to purchase the business in 19X5. Liquidity did decline to 80% due to the loan from the Corporation to the Officers. But, again, Net Profit totalled $12,060 which is much more than enough to meet those long term loan payments of $3,600 per year.

The Accountant is in the process of preparing Financial Statements as of June 30, 19X9 and indications are that Sales for 19X9 will be $245,000 and Net Profit will be close to $10,000 after Taxes.

An interesting and unusual feature of the Balance Sheet is the abundance of "Cash on Deposit" which was $24,188 in June, 19X8. This excessive cash position was temporary, and resulted from a Summer Sale to clean out Inventory.

Note that Accounts Receivable of $5,976 are quite small in relation to Sales of $231,195. This is another indication of the business "smartness" of Jack Adams — he sells mostly for Cash and there are relatively few Charge Accounts (Receivables) to worry about. Also, June would be one of the seasonal low points in the department store business. So Cash is nicely available to help purchase additional merchandise for the coming Fall Season.

Everyone concerned, including The Small Business Administration, is most pleased with the progress of this small enterprise under the energetic and capable management of Jack Adams.

QUESTIONS ON CHAPTER XIII:

1. Describe and comment on the Three C's of Credit. What do we mean by Character, Capacity, and Capital?

2. Under what circumstances is it possible to lend financial aid to "Certain Small Businessess?"

3. Point out several of the hazards and problems of Small Business.

4. Can you Reconcile Working Capital between 19X7 and 19X8 in the Gilbert Department Store statements?

CHAPTER XIV

Another in the select group of Special Financial Statements

Away back in the Great Depression Year of 1931, young Bernard Gellin started to sell fishing tackle, fishing rods, hooks, lines, and sinkers to hardware stores in Hartford, Connecticut. He operated from his father's home with starting Capital of maybe $200 and a tiny stock of merchandise obtained on credit. Certainly, he was the littlest of Small Businessmen. Bernie would trudge on foot from store to store in heat, rain, and snow, peddling his wares. His personality and determination were his Assets in those beginning days, and he gradually built up an increasing volume of business. As the years sped past, the American Economy began to recover from the Great Depression of the 1930's, and Bernie was right there ready to take advantage of new business and more sales created by our expanding economy. Not only was consumer purchasing power on the up-swing, but the American people in general began to have more leisure time away from the job than ever before. This meant just one fortunate thing to Bernie — people had more time "to go fishin'."

As his business grew, more Capital in the form of Bank Loans was needed to support the increasing sales volume. Now began Bernie's ordeal in his search for financial help. His present Bank refused to increase its loans beyond $15,000, but Bernie needed at least $30,000 in bank loans. He was finally introduced to another Banker, and after a "Plant Visitation" and Analysis, this Banker agreed to a Capital Loan of $40,000.

The remarkable growth of this Small Business is dramatically pictured in the following Financial Statement Analysis:

TAYLOR AND FRANCIS

CERTIFIED PUBLIC ACCOUNTANTS

HARTFORD, CONN.

April 15, 1977

Mr. Bernard Gellin
Gellin Company
171 Maple Avenue
Hartford, Connecticut

Dear Sir:

In accordance with your request, we audited the books and records of Bernard Gellin Company for the year ending December 31, 1976, and herewith submit the following:

Exhibit A — Balance Sheet as at December 31, 1976.

Exhibit B — Statement of Profit and Loss for the year ending December 31, 1976.

The merchandise inventory in the amount of $118,041.85, as shown in Exhibit A, was submitted to us.

The accounts receivable as at December 31, 1976 were confirmed by means of the negative confirmation method. The debtors were requested to advise your Auditors of any exceptions to the balances as indicated on the statements mailed to them. The replies received by your Auditors indicated some exceptions which were not significant and do not require comment in this report.

All other facts and figures contained in this report were compiled directly from the books and records of the company without resorting to outside verification of any of the accounts by correspondence.

Respectfully submitted,

Taylor & Francis
CERTIFIED PUBLIC ACCOUNTANT

BERNARD GELLIN COMPANY

HARTFORD, CONNECTICUT

BALANCE SHEET

December 31, 1976

ASSETS

Current Assets:

Cash in Bank	$ 16,116.40	
Cash on Hand	200.00	
Accounts Receivable - Trade	94,402.52	
Accounts Receivable - Employees	128.83	
Merchandise Inventory	118,041.85	
Total Current Assets		$228,889.60

Fixed Assets:	Cost	Reserve For Depreciation	Book Value	
Furniture, Fixtures and Equipment	$10,927.17	$4,921.34	$6,005.83	
Automobile	2,806.55	2,455.74	350.81	
	$13,733.72	$7,377.08		6,356.64

Deferred Charges:		
Security on Lease	650.00	
Unexpired Insurance	638.42	1,288.42

Other Assets:	
Loans Receivable	300.00

TOTAL ASSETS	$236,834.66

LIABILITIES and CAPITAL

Current Liabilities:

Accounts Payable - Trade	$ 46,976.59	
Accounts Payable - Other	97.20	
Notes Payable - Bank	2,000.00	
Commissions Payable	224.17	
Taxes Payable and Accrued	1,537.91	
Expenses Accrued	1,402.50	
Total Current Liabilities		$ 52,238.37

Capital:

Bernard Gellin, Net Worth - 1/1/76	$160,473.27	
Add: Net Profit for Year	57,847.23	
	$218,320.50	

Less: Drawings	$ 13,541.31		
Federal Income Taxes			
Paid	19,875.90		
Donations	307.00	33,724.21	
Net Worth - December 31, 1976			184,596.29

TOTAL LIABILITIES and CAPITAL $236,834.66

BERNARD GELLIN COMPANY

HARTFORD, CONNECTICUT

STATEMENT OF PROFIT AND LOSS

For The Year Ending December 31, 1976

Income from Sales:

Ammunition and Guns		$315,198.76	
Fishing Tackle and Miscellaneous		509,077.41	
		$824,276.17	
Less: Sales Discounts	$ 12,736.52		
Trade Discounts	7,477.84	20,214.36	
Net Sales			$804,061.81

Cost of Sales:

Inventory - January 1, 1976		110,912.74	
Purchases - Ammunition and Guns	$281,714.46		
Purchases - Fishing Tackle and Miscellaneous	390,144.28	671,858.74	
Freight In		7,688.81	
		$790,460.29	
Less: Inventory - December 31, 1976		118,041.85	
Cost of Goods Sold			672,418.44
Gross Profit			$131,643.37

Operating Expenses:

Sales Expenses:

Commissions - Salesmen	$ 25,314.64	
Advertising	1,568.23	
Bad Debts	295.74	
Total Sales Expenses		$ 27,178.61

Store and Shipping Expenses:

Salaries	$ 22,263.67	
Freight Out	3,647.25	
Supplies	2,836.51	
Rent	4,828.75	
Buying Expense	457.11	
Heat and Lights	1,016.44	
Maintenance and Repairs	1,070.54	
Window Cleaning	112.00	
Rubbish Removal	80.00	
Alarm System	77.76	
Total Store and Shipping Expenses		$ 36,390.03

BERNARD GELLIN COMPANY

HARTFORD, CONNECTICUT

STATEMENT OF PROFIT AND LOSS

For The Year Ending December 31, 1976

Gross Profit - Brought Forward		$131,643.37
Operating Expenses - Continued		
General and Office Expenses:		
Office Salaries	$ 10,327.44	
Interest	1,265.89	
Postage	2,196.50	
Telephone	2,323.08	
Accounting and Legal	1,490.50	
Taxes	1,933.09	
Office Expense and Supplies	76.46	
General Expenses	588.97	
Insurance	2,792.14	
Dues and Subscriptions	100.00	
Credit Service	536.45	
Depreciation	1,885.34	
Total General and Office Expenses	$ 25,515.86	
Total Operating Expenses		$ 89,084.50
Operating Profit		$ 42,558.87
Other Income:		
Discounts on Purchases	$ 14,937.00	
Bad Debts Recovered	41.70	
Miscellaneous Income	309.66	
Total Other Income		$ 15,288.36
NET PROFIT		$ 57,847.23

Eventually the business year was changed from a calendar year end of December 31st to a fiscal year end of November 30th, and the business was Incorporated.

TAYLOR AND FRANCIS

CERTIFIED PUBLIC ACCOUNTANTS

Hartford, Conn. 06103

February 6, 1988

Mr. Bernard Gellin
Bernard Gellin Co., Inc.
Hartford, Connecticut

Dear Sir:

In accordance with your request, we examined the books and records of your company for the year ended November 30, 1987, and herewith submit the following:

Exhibit A — Balance Sheet as at November 30, 1987.

Exhibit B — Statement of Profit and Loss for the year ended November 30, 1987.

Schedule No. 1 — Schedule of Operating Expenses for the year ended November 30, 1987.

The merchandise inventory totalling $567,914.20 was submitted to us.

This report was compiled from the books and records of your company without outside verification. We examined or tested the accounting records of the corporation and other supporting evidence and made a general review of the accounting methods. However, our examination was not sufficient in scope to enable us to render an opinion upon the financial statements.

Respectfully submitted,

Taylor and Francis

Certified Public Accountants

120

Author's Note:

This is an excellent example of the value of an Accountant's Report. An Accountant is prepared to make two types of Financial Reports for his client:

1. A complete Audit in depth—wherein the correctness of Accounts Receivable are verified by letters to a large percentage of customers; bank deposits and loans are confirmed; most Accounts Payable are verified by letter; and the method of valuing Inventory at Cost or Market Value, whichever is less, is observed by the Accountant. If all confirmations are substantially correct, the Accountant will "Certify" the Financial Statements over his signature. Although more expensive, this is the type of Audit and Report that we all like to see—this lends credibility and confidence to the business which is under Analysis.

2. An incomplete examination of the books and records of the business wherein the management did **not** request confirmation and verification of important Assets and Liabilities. Therefore, the Accountant will **not** "Certify" the Financial Statements, and will not express an opinion as to the accuracy of the Statements as a whole.

   Unfortunately, the majority of Small Businessmen do not ask their accountants for "Certification" of his Financial Report. More often than not, then, the Analyst must depend on the Honesty and Character of the man, the person behind the cold financial figures.

BERNARD GELLIN CO., INC.

BALANCE SHEET

November 30, 1987

ASSETS

Current Assets:

Cash in Bank and On Hand		$ 20,673.99
Accounts Receivable	$557,162.56	
Less: Reserve for Bad Debts	6,445.78	550,716.78
Merchandise Inventory		567,914.20
Prepaid Expenses		2,466.00
Accounts Receivable - Other		2,894.48
Total Current Assets		$1,144,665.45

Fixed Assets:

Furniture and Fixtures	$ 46,578.73	
Automobiles	3,412.69	
Improvements	4,353.78	
	$ 54,345.20	
Less: Accumulated Depreciation	31,872.56	22,472.64
		$1,167,138.09

LIABILITIES and CAPITAL

Current Liabilities:

Accounts Payable	$270,796.54
Notes Payable - Bank	245,000.00
Loan Payable - B. Gellin	44,500.00
Employee Bond Deductions	36.75

Accrued Liabilities:

Taxes Payable and Accrued	60,565.48
Officers' Salaries	30,250.00
Commissions	16,245.32
Interest	4,653.27
Other	1,322.00
Total Current Liabilities	$ 673,369.36

Capital:

Capital Stock Issued		$140,000.00	
Earned Surplus - 12/1/86	$290,150.96		
Add: Net Profit for Year			
Ended 11/30/87	63,617.77	353,768.73	493,768.73
			$1,167,138.09

BERNARD GELLIN CO., INC.

STATEMENT OF PROFIT AND LOSS

For the Year Ended November 30, 1987

Income from Sales:

Guns and Ammunition	$1,952,594.34	
Other Sales	740,728.17	$2,693,322.51
Less: Cash Discounts		43,045.06
Net Sales		$2,650,277.45

Cost of Sales:

Inventory, December 1, 1986	$ 562,775.33	
Purchases - Guns and Ammunition	1,692,565.24	
Purchases - Other	572,952.68	
Freight In	7,729.10	
	$2,836,022.35	
Less: Discounts on Purchases	52,762.94	
	$2,783,259.41	
Less: Inventory, November 30, 1987	567,914.20	
Cost of Goods Sold		2,215,345.21
Gross Profit		$ 434,932.24

Operating Expenses:

Sales Expenses	$ 86,802.46	
Warehouse and Shipping	117,031.45	
General and Office	126,145.04	
Total Operating Expenses		329,978.95
Operating Profit		$ 104,953.29

Other Income:

Interest Income	$ 398.80	
Miscellaneous	8,471.54	
Total Other Income		8,870.34
Net Profit - Before Federal and State Income Tax		$ 113,823.63
Less: Federal Income Tax	$ 44,180.98	
State Corporation Business Tax	6,024.88	50,205.86
Net Profit - Transferred to Surplus		$ 63,617.77

TAYLOR AND FRANCIS

CERTIFIED PUBLIC ACCOUNTANTS

HARTFORD, CONN. 06103

February 13, 1989

Mr. Bernard Gellin
Bernard Gellin Co., Inc.
Hartford, Connecticut

Dear Sir:

In accordance with your request, we examined the books and records of your company for the year ended November 30, 1988, and herewith submit the following:

> Exhibit A — Balance Sheet as at November 30, 1988.
>
> Exhibit B — Statement of Profit and Loss for the year ended November 30, 1988.
>
> Schedule No. 1 — Schedule of Operating Expenses for the year ended November 30, 1988.

The merchandise inventory totaling $699,126.93 was submitted to us.

As the scope of our examination was limited, an opinion upon the financial statements of your company is not being rendered.

Respectfully submitted,

TAYLOR AND FRANCIS
Certified Public Accountants

126

BERNARD GELLIN CO., INC.

BALANCE SHEET

November 30, 1988

ASSETS

Current Assets:

Cash in Bank and on Hand	$ 13,825.45	
Accounts Receivable	$503,790.74	
Less: Reserve for Bad Debts	6,445.78	497,344.96
Merchandise Inventory		699,126.93
Prepaid Expenses		614.00
Accounts Receivable - Other		1,155.78
Total Current Assets		$1,212,067.12

Fixed Assets:

Furniture and Fixtures	$ 49,092.75	
Automobile	3,412.69	
Improvements	4,353.78	
	$ 56,859.22	
Less: Accumulated Depreciation	36,091.42	20,767.80
		$1,232,834.92

LIABILITIES AND CAPITAL

Current Liabilities:

Accounts Payable	$ 266,785.59	
Notes Payable - Bank	178,000.00	
Loan Payable - B. Gellin	42,500.00	
Employee Bond Deductions	80.00	

Accrued Liabilities:

Taxes Payable and Accrued	108,264.25	
Officers' Salaries	30,500.00	
Commissions	2,888.65	
Interest	8,136.77	
Other	3,006.00	
Total Current Liabilities		$ 640,161.26

Capital:

Capital Stock Issued	$ 140,000.00	
Earned Surplus -		
December 1, 1987 $353,768.73		

Add: Net Profit for **Year Ended**		
November 30, 1988 98,904.93		
Earned Surplus - November 30, 1988	452,673.66	
Total Capital		592,673.66
		$1,232,834.92

BERNARD GELLIN CO., INC.

STATEMENT OF PROFIT AND LOSS

For the Year Ended November 30, 1988

Income from Sales:

Guns and Ammunition	$2,182,747.33
Other Sales	977,233.87
Total Sales	$3,159,981.20
Less: Cash Discounts	54,727.00
Net Sales	$3,105,254.20

Cost of Sales:

Inventory, December 1, 1987	$ 567,914.20	
Purchases -		
Guns and Ammunition	1,959,424.81	
Purchases - Other	795,599.93	
Freight In	7,650.36	
	$3,330,589.30	
Less: Discounts on Purchases	83,314.68	
	$3,247,274.62	
Less: Inventory,		
November 30, 1988	699,126.93	
Cost of Sales		2,548,147.69
Gross Profit		$ 557,106.51

Operating Expenses:

Sales Expense	$ 88,962.86	
Warehouse and Shipping	128,226.98	
General and Office	141,363.20	
Total Operating Expenses		358,553.04
Operating Profit		$ 198,553.47

Other Income:

Interest Income	$ 367.98	
Miscellaneous	3,691.25	
Bad Debts Recovered	280.05	
Total Other Income		4,339.28
Net Profit - Before Federal and State Income Taxes		$ 202,892.75
Less: Federal Income Tax	$ 93,393.03	
State Corporation Business Tax	10,594.79	103,987.82
Net Profit Transferred to Surplus		$ 98,904.93

Now, the spread of the figures from 1976 through 1988, a twelve year span:

BERNARD GELLIN CO., INC.

WHOLESALE SPORTING GOODS AND FIREARMS

	Dec. 31, 1976	Nov. 30, 1987	Nov. 30, 1988
Current Assets	$228,889	$1,144,665	$1,212,067
Current Liabilities	52,238	673,369	640,161
Working Capital	176,651	471,296	571,906
Equipment and Other Assets Net	7,945	22,472	20,767
Total Assets	236,835	1,167,138	1,232,834
Capital Stock	———	140,000	140,000
Surplus	———	353,768	452,673
Net Worth	184,596	493,768	592,673
Sales	804,061	2,650,277	3,105,254
Net Profit after Taxes	57,847	63,617	98,904
Net Worth Increase	———	309,172 (11 years)	98,904

Ratios:

Current Ratio	4 to 1	1.6 to 1	2 to 1
Liquidity	210%	114%	80%
Average Collection Period	42 days	75 days	57 days
Debt to Worth	28%	136%	108%
Inventory Turnover	6.7 times	4.6 times	4.4 times
Net Profit on Sales after Taxes	7%	2.4%	3%

Comments:

These twelve year Comparisons and Ratios are a remarkable and vivid panorama of not only the growth and expansion of this business, but also the added problems, the stress and strain that go along hand in hand with tremendous increases in sales volume, and "Success" in general. The financial paradox is that the more business you do, the greater is the need for more Capital, or Loans, and the greater are your Income Taxes. In 1988, Net Profit before Taxes was $202,892; now deduct **$103,987** Income Taxes for Net Profit of $98,904. Over **One half** of Net Profit was siphoned off in Income Taxes.

Between 1987 and 1988, Net Worth gained by $98,904 which was exactly the amount of Net Profit for 1988, and this Reconciles the Net Worth change.

Working Capital Reconciliation:

Working Capital 1988	**$571,906**
Working Capital 1987	471,296
Working Capital Increase	100,610
Incoming Net Proift 1988	98,905
Add Decrease in Fixed Assets	1,705
Working Capital Increase	100,610

Thus, in 1988 we were pleased to see that no substantial additions to Equipment and Fixtures (Fixed Assets) were necessary. Depreciation of those Fixed Assets in 1988 resulted in a net decline of $1,705 in the value of Fixed Assets which went into Working Capital thereby increasing Working Capital over and above Net Profit coming into the Balance Sheet. "Any Decrease in Fixed Assets causes an Increase in Working Capital above the Line."

The year ended December 31, 1976, was the best for Bernie. Sales were a comfortable $804,000, with a handsome Net Profit of $57,800. As a Proprietor in 1976, Bernie paid an Income Tax of $19,875 which left $37,925 in the business. Although sales in 1988 were almost four times sales in 1976, Net Profit retained in the business after Taxes was only about two and one-half times that of 1976.

In that happy year of 1976, note that Bernie needed a small bank loan of only $2,000, but in 1988 bank loans had increased to $178,000! Because of the tremendous increase in sales volume, Inventory, and Accounts Receivable were over one million dollars in 1988.

Note that both Working Capital and Net Worth have gained and increased nicely through the years under review as the result of the retention of Net Profits after Taxes.

All of this "Success" is reflected dramatically in the Ratios. In 1976, all the Ratios were away above normal, as Cash plus Accounts Receivable were more than double Current Liabilities, and Debt was only 28% of Net Worth. In 1988, Liquidity had declined to 80% (Cash plus Receivables fell short of covering Current Liabilities), and Debt was 8% in excess of Net Worth. All of this is a vivid picture of the financial stress and strain that comes with a remarkably large increase in sales volume on Capital (Net Worth) which is held down by heavy Income Taxes.

Nevertheless, this successful business continued in good shape by modern financial standards. A bank loan of $200,000 would be quite reasonable because it was less than 1/2 of Working Capital, and considerably less than 1/2 of Net Worth.

CHAPTER XV

A THIRD VERY SPECIAL FINANCIAL STATEMENT

In the City of Waterbury, Connecticut, at the end of World War II in 1945, Frank A. Grasso had received his Honorable Discharge from the U. S. Navy, and had returned to his job as a salesman of electrical supplies, calling on industrial factories and electrical construction contractors. Frank had made many real business friends throughout Connecticut, and it was inevitable that one day he would finally leave his employer and "go into business for himself." Frank and his brother John somehow scraped together $10,000 in cash Capital which was nowhere near enough to enter the very competitive wholesale electrical supply business, and to fight older, established, well capitalized companies.

The beginning months and years were, indeed, a nightmare of obstacles, problems, and frustrations. Nationally known manufacturers of electrical supplies were hesitant to sell to the new Frank A. Grasso Co., Inc., and Frank's competitors did all they could to try to force manufacturers not to sell to Grasso. In fact, Frank had to buy many supplies from other out-of-state friendly wholesalers.

Also, this baby corporation did not qualify for much in unsecured bank loans, although one banker did grant a loan of $5,000 which was one half of the company's starting Capital. With all these difficulties it is hard to see how the Grassos survived; gradually sales increased and small profits began to appear. On the basis of this rather encouraging progress, the bank increased its loans to $8,500, and Frank and John had their foothold in a growing business.

JONES, EVERETT & FRANKLIN

CERTIFIED PUBLIC ACCOUNTANTS

Frank A. Grasso, Inc.
31 Pope Park Highway
Waterbury, Connecticut

We have made an interim examination of the accounts of Frank A. Grasso, Inc. for the six months ended April 30, 19X2 and present the following financial statements, based on an estimated inventory.

EXHIBIT "A" Balance Sheet as at April 30, 19X2.

EXHIBIT "B" Statement of Income and Accumulated

Earnings for the Six Months Ended

April 30, 19X2.

COMMENTS

The inventory of merchandise was estimated on the basis of 19% gross profit ratio which was the experience of the preceding year. This gave an estimated inventory of $66,475.00 or about $4,000.00 more than the physical inventory of October 31, 19X1.

A listing of the customers' accounts receivable according to age was prepared by the bookkeeper and test-checked by us. We considered the reserve for doubtful accounts to be adequate.

All applicable taxes were accrued, including $1,900.00 for Federal and State Income Taxes for the current period.

Working Capital increased $2,543.70 during the six months' period as accounted for below:

	4/4/X2	10/31/X1	Increase
Summary of Working Capital:			
Current Assets	$123,869.41	$128,428.39	$4,558.98
Current Liabilities	47,325.34	54,428.02	7,102.68
Working Capital	$ 76,544.07	$ 74,000.37	$2,543.70

Factors accounting for this net increase were:

Increases in Working Capital:

Net Profit for the period, per Exhibit "B"	$3,412.01	
Add: Depreciation (a non-cash expense)	1,577.37	
Total Increases (Provided by operations)		$4,989.38

Decreases in Working Capital:

Purchase of automobile	1,005.98	
Purchase of accounting machine	1,351.50	
Other furniture and alterations	88.20	
Total Decreases (Applied to purchase of fixed assets)		2,445.68
Net Increase in Working Capital		$2,543.70

Operations for the period are set forth in detail on Exhibit "B." The result was a profit of $3,412.01 after a provision of $1,900.00 for current income taxes.

Jones, Everett & Franklin

Certified Public Accountants

FRANK A. GRASSO, INC.

BALANCE SHEET AS AT APRIL 30, 19X2

ASSETS

CURRENT ASSETS:

Cash on deposit and on hand		$ 3,173.00
Accounts receivable - trade	$56,522.62	
Less: Reserve for doubtful accounts	4,427.15	52,095.47
Note receivable - trade customer		1,147.00
Merchandise inventory		66,475.85
Prepaid insurance and interest		978.09
TOTAL CURRENT ASSETS		**$123,869.41**

FIXED ASSETS:

Automobiles and truck	10,968.85	
Less: Reserve for depreciation	2,053.16	8,915.69
Furniture, fixtures and alterations	6,389.18	
Less: Reserve for depreciation	1,927.48	4,461.70
DEPRECIATED COST - FIXED ASSETS		13,377.39
TOTAL ASSETS		**$137,246.80**

LIABILITIES AND STOCKHOLDERS' EQUITY

CURRENT LIABILITIES:

Accounts Payable	31,850.30
Note Payable - bank short term	2,500.00
Loans payable - officers	8,000.00
Accrued Social Security Taxes	193.13
Employees' Income Tax withheld	352.00
Accrued Federal Income Taxes - 19X1	1,722.37

Accrued Federal and State Income Taxes - current period	1,900.00	
Accrued property taxes	422.14	
Accrued Connecticut Sales Tax	385.40	

TOTAL CURRENT LIABILITIES 47,325.34

NOTE PAYABLE - BANK - LONG TERM 5,000.00

STOCKHOLDERS' EQUITY:

Capital Stock - Common:	35,000.00	
Accumulated earnings, per Exhibit "B"	49,921.46	

TOTAL STOCKHOLDERS' EQUITY 84,921.46

TOTAL LIABILITIES AND STOCKHOLDERS' EQUITY $137,246.80

EXHIBIT "B"

FRANK A. GRASSO, INC.

STATEMENT OF INCOME AND ACCUMULATED EARNINGS

FOR THE SIX MONTHS ENDED APRIL 30, 19X2

GROSS SALES		$255,306.72
Less: Returns and allowances		4,359.83

NET SALES 250,946.89

COST OF GOODS SOLD: (Condensed)

Merchandise	$202,303.21	
Transportation in	963.77	

TOTAL COST OF GOODS SOLD 203,266.98

GROSS PROFIT (estimated at 19%) 47,679.91

SELLING EXPENSE:

Salary - sales manager	2,145.00
Salaries - salesmen	8,008.00
Salaries - countermen and warehouse	5,746.00
Salaries - trucker	1,409.44
Auto and truck expenses	1,845.13
Travel and entertainment	2,419.41
Transportation out	163.14
Advertising	378.00
Commissions allowed	255.21
Miscellaneous	1,572.43
TOTAL SELLING EXPENSE	23,941.76

ADMINISTRATIVE EXPENSE:

Salaries - officers	6,097.00
Salaries - office	3,072.00
Rent	1,986.00
Light and power	261.89
Insurance	792.82
Taxes - payroll	481.19
Taxes - City and miscellaneous	560.69
Telephone and telegraph	635.99
Stationery, postage and office supplies	547.40
Association dues and subscriptions	296.97
Legal and accounting services	225.00
Contributions	58.00
General expense	554.33
Depreciation	1,577.37

TOTAL ADMINISTRATIVE EXPENSE   17,146.65

TOTAL OPERATING EXPENSES   41,088.41

NET OPERATING PROFIT - forwarded $ 6,591.50

FRANK A. GRASSO, INC.

STATEMENT OF INCOME AND ACCUMULATED EARNINGS

FOR THE SIX MONTHS ENDED APRIL 30, 19X2

NET OPERATING PROFIT - brought forward		$ 6,591.50
OTHER INCOME:		
Cash discounts earned		5,709.98
		12,301.48
OTHER DEDUCTIONS:		
Cash discounts allowed	$ 4,369.40	
Interest	174.07	
Officers' life insurance premiums	2,446.00	
TOTAL OTHER DEDUCTIONS		6,989.47
NET PROFIT, before provision for Income Taxes		5,312.01
PROVISION FOR FEDERAL AND STATE INCOME TAXES		1,900.00
NET PROFIT FOR THE PERIOD SIX MONTHS		3,412.01
ACCUMULATED EARNINGS, October 31, 19X1		46,509.45
ACCUMULATED EARNINGS, April 30, 19X2		$ 49,921.46

JONES, EVERETT & FRANKLIN

CERTIFIED PUBLIC ACCOUNTANTS

The Board of Directors

Frank A. Grasso, Inc.:

We have examined the balance sheet of Frank A. Grasso, Inc. as of October 31, 19X7 and the related statement of earnings and retained earnings for the year then ended. Our examination was made in accordance with generally accepted auditing standards, and accordingly included such tests of the accounting records and such other auditing procedures as we considered necessary in the circumstances.

In our opinion, the accompanying balance sheet and statement of earnings and retained earnings present fairly the financial position of Frank A. Grasso, Inc. as October 31, 19X7 and the results of its operations for the year then ended, in conformity with generally accepted accounting principles applied on a basis consistent with that of the preceding year.

JONES, EVERETT & FRANKLIN
CERTIFIED PUBLIC ACCOUNTANTS

December 27, 19X7

Author's Note:

We must assume that the CPA's have confirmed and verified important Assets and Liabilities. Therefore, they have "Certified" the correctness and accuracy of the Statement as a whole.

FRANK A. GRASSO, INC.

BALANCE SHEET (Pennies Omitted)

OCTOBER 31, 19X7

ASSETS

Current Assets:

Cash	$ 11,649
Accounts receivable	286,570
Less allowance for doubtful accounts	11,063
Net accounts receivable	275,507
Inventory, at lower of cost or market	213,157
Prepaid insurance	579
Total current assets	500,892

Property and equipment:

Automobiles and trucks	26,903
Furniture, fixtures and equipment	9,237
Leasehold improvements	16,429
	52,569
Less accumulated depreciation	26,905
Net Property and equipment	25,664

Other assets:

Cash surrender value - life insurance	40,794
	$567,350

LIABILITIES AND STOCKHOLDERS' EQUITY

Current Liabilities:

Note payable - bank	$ ——
Notes payable - other	18,000
Accounts payable	133,861
Accrued salaries	35,243
Accrued payroll, property, and sales tax	7,222
Employees' taxes withheld	1,064
Accrued interest payable	1,545
Federal and State income taxes payable	27,896
Total current liabilities	224,831

Long-term debt:

Notes payable - principal stockholder	45,000

Stockholders' equity:

Common Stock	95,000
Retained earnings	218,773
	313,773
Less cost of 75 shares in treasury	16,254
Total stockholders' equity	297,519
	$567,350

FRANK A. GRASSO, INC.

STATEMENT OF EARNINGS AND RETAINED EARNINGS

YEAR ENDED OCTOBER 31, 19X7

Gross sales	$1,946,381
Less returns and allowances	23,603
Net Sales	1,922,778
Cost of goods sold: (Condensed)	
Merchandise	1,581,418
Transportation in	1,335
	1,582,753
Gross profit	340,025
Selling, general and administrative expenses	271,675
Net operating profit	68,350
Other income:	
Cash discounts earned	26,724
Excess of cash value increase over premiums paid on life insurance	267
	26,991
	95,341
Other deductions:	
Cash discounts allowed	22,731
Interest	6,920
Contributions	1,365
	31,016

Net profit before provision for Federal income taxes	64,325
Provision for Federal income taxes	24,248
Net income for the year	40,077
Retained earnings at beginning of year	178,696
Retained earnings at end of year	218,773

SCHEDULE 3

FRANK A. GRASSO, INC.

Source and Application of Funds

Year Ended October 31, 19X7

Funds provided:	
Net earnings	$ 40,077
Increase in long-term debt	2,000
Depreciation - non-cash expense	7,514
Total funds provided	49,591
Funds used:	
To Purchase fixed assets	7,977
Increase in cash value of life insurance	2,799
Total funds used	10,776
Net increase to working capital	$ 38,815

FRANK A. GRASSO, INC.

Selling, General and Administrative Expenses

Year ended October 31, 19X7

Selling expenses:	
Salaries - general manager 1/2	$ 13,520
Salaries - salesmen	71,240
Salaries - counter and warehouse	48,379
Salaries - truckers	11,800
Auto and truck expenses	6,878
Travel and entertainment	9,323
Transportation out	1,170
Advertising	996
Miscellaneous	3,818
	167,124
General and administrative expenses:	
Salaries - officers	27,170
Salaries - office	19,140
Rent	11,700
Light and Power	1,578
Insurance	6,712
Depreciation	7,514
Taxes - payroll	5,542
Taxes - city	5,377
Connecticut corporation business tax	3,642
Telephone and telegraph	5,323
Stationery, postage and office supplies	4,686
Association dues and subscriptions	2,318
Legal and accounting	1,214
General expense	2,635
	104,551
	$271,675

JONES, EVERETT & FRANKLIN
CERTIFIED PUBLIC ACCOUNTANTS

The Board of Directors

Frank A. Grasso, Inc.:

We have examined the balance sheet of Frank A. Grasso, Inc. as of October 31, 19X8 and the related statement of earnings and retained earnings for the year then ended. Our examination was made in accordance with generally accepted auditing standards, and accordingly included such tests of the accounting records and such other auditing procedures as we considered necessary in the circumstances.

In our opinion, the accompanying balance sheet and statement of earnings and retained earnings present fairly the financial position of Frank A. Grasso, Inc. at October 31, 19X8 and the results of its operations for the year then ended, in conformity with generally accepted accounting principles applied on a basis consistent with that of the preceding year.

JONES, EVERETT & FRANKLIN
CERTIFIED PUBLIC ACCOUNTANTS

January 3, 19X9

EXHIBIT A

FRANK A. GRASSO, INC.

BALANCE SHEET

OCTOBER 31, 19X8

ASSETS

Current assets:

Cash	$ 9,898
Accounts receivable	264,691
Less allowance for doubtful accounts	11,878

148

Net accounts receivable	$ 252,813
Inventory, at lower of cost or market	216,324
Prepaid insurance	608
Total Current Assets	479,643

Property and equipment:

Automobiles and trucks	28,191
Furniture, fixtures and equipment	7,208
Leasehold improvements	16,429
	51,828
Less accumulated depreciation	27,786
Net property and equipment	24,042

Other assets:

Cash surrender value - life insurance	43,572
	$ 547,257

LIABILITIES AND STOCKHOLDERS' EQUITY

Current Liabilities:

Notes Payable - other	$ 7,000
Accounts Payable	90,764
Accrued salaries	38,666
Accrued payroll, property and sales tax	7,034
Employees' taxes withheld	—
Accrued expenses	2,993
Federal and state income taxes payable	27,258
Total current liabilities	173,715

Long-term debt:

Notes payable - principal stockholder	40,000

Stockholders' equity:

Common stock	95,000
Retained earnings	254,796
	349,796

Less cost of 75 shares in treasury	16,254
Total stockholders' equity	333,542
	$ 547,257

FRANK A. GRASSO, INC.

STATEMENT OF EARNINGS AND RETAINED EARNINGS

YEAR ENDED OCTOBER 31, 19X8

Gross sales	$2,057,517
Less returns and allowances	19,077
Net Sales	2,038,440
Cost of goods sold: (Condensed)	
Merchandise	1,686,270
Transportation in	1,409
	1,687,679
Gross profit	350,761
Selling, general and administrative expenses	290,870
Net operating profit	59,891
Other income:	
Cash discounts earned	27,729
Excess of cash value increase over premiums paid on life insurance	358
	28,087
	87,978

Other deductions:

Cash discounts allowed	21,906
Interest	5,572
Contributions	540
	28,018

Net profit before provision for Federal income taxes	59,960
Provision for Federal income taxes	23,937
Net income for the year	36,023
Retained earnings at beginning of year	218,773
Retained earnings at end of year	$ 254,796

SCHEDULE 3

FRANK A. GRASSO, INC.

SOURCE AND APPLICATION OF FUNDS

YEAR ENDED OCTOBER 31, 19X8

Funds provided:

Net earnings	$ 36,023
Depreciation - noncash expense	8,346
Total funds provided	44,369

Funds used:

To purchase fixed assets	6,724
Increase in cash value of life insurance	2,778
Decrease in long-term debt	5,000
Total funds used	14,502
Net increase in working capital	$ 29,867

ANALYSIS FRANK A. GRASSO, INC.

	April 30,19XX*	Oct. 31,19X7	Oct. 31, 19X8
Current assets	123,869	500,892	479,643
Current Liabilities	47,325	224,831	173,715
Working Capital	76,544	276,061	305,928
Fixed Assets Net	13,377	66,458	67,614
Total Assets	137,246	567,350	547,257
Sales (6 months)	250,946	1,922,778	2,038,440
Net profit after Taxes	3,412	40,077	36,023
Officers' Salaries	6,097	26,000	40,000
Capital Stock	35,000	95,000	95,000
Surplus	49,921	218,773	254,796
Net Worth †	84,921	313,773	349,796
Net Worth Gain	—	228,852	36,023
		(17 years)	

RATIOS:

Current Ratio	2.6 to 1	2.2 to 1	2.7 to 1
Liquidity	116%	128%	150%
Debt to Worth	60%	80%	60%
Average Collection Period	36 Days	50 Days	39 Days
Inventory Turnover	3.7 times	9 times	9 times
	(6 mos.)		
Net Profit on Sales	1.2%	2%	1.8%

Comments:

The Fixed Asset in 19X8 of "Cash Surrender Value Life Insurance" is, indeed, a valuable Asset. This represents accumulated Cash Value over the years in several Life Insurance Policies on the lives of all four Officers of the Corporation and the Beneficiary is the company, Frank A. Grasso, Inc. Upon the death of any Officer, the Cor-

---

* Date is twenty-seven years before the second analysis in 19X7.

† Deduct "Leasehold Improvements" to arrive at "Tangible Net Worth."

poration will receive the face amount of the Policy in cash which may be used to purchase the Capital Stock in Grasso, Inc. from the deceased Estate. This very important matter of taking out Life Insurance on key Officers is all too often neglected by Small Business management. The Analyst is surprised, more often than not, but pleased to see this type of Life Insurance which helps to assure the peaceful continuity of the Corporation.

The item of $16,254 "Cost of 75 shares of Stock in Treasury" indicates that some Stockholders, perhaps needing cash, sold some of their stock back to Frank A. Grasso, Inc., and the Corporation holds that Stock in its Vault for possible resale at a later date. Since this is a reduction, or retirement of Capital Stock, the $16,254 must be subtracted from Corporate Net Worth.

Another item of interest is the $40,000 Note Payable Long Term to Principal Stockholder (Frank Grasso). This represents money loaned to his Corporation by Frank with no specific repayment schedule. Back in 19X6, a Statement showed that the Corporation was borrowing $40,000 from its bank. Over the years, frugal Frank has saved considerable money and asked himself "why should the Corporation pay interest to the bank? I will loan my Company the money, and I will collect the interest."

Nice thinking, Frank.

Note that Working Capital gained only $29,867 in spite of a Net Profit of $36,023.

WORKING CAPITAL RECONCILIATION

Working Capital 19X8 —	$305,928
Working Capital 19X7 —	276,061
Working Capital Gain =	29,867
Incoming Net Profit 19X8 —	36,023
Less Pay Down Long Term Debt —	5,000
	31,023
Less Increase in Fixed Assets —	1,156
	$ 29,867

An Increase in Fixed Assets will Decrease Working Capital. A Decrease in Long Term Debt below the Line will Decrease Working Capital.

As between 19X7 and 19X8, Net Worth Gain of $36,023 is Reconciled quickly because that Gain precisely equals Net Profit for 19X8 of $36,023.

In the eighteen year period under review, the outstanding feature is the consistent, steady Liquidity as shown by the Ratios — Cash plus Accounts Receivable always more than covered Current Liabilities. Also, the Current Ratio was steady at better than 2 to 1. The Company did not need bank loans, which is quite remarkable these days. The answers to this unusually happy state of financial affairs are to be found in the rapid turnover of Inventory of 9 times in 19X8, plus a relatively short Collection Period of Receivables of less than 40 days. In other words, Inventory was sold rapidly and the majority of Receivables were collected promptly allowing Grasso, Inc. to discount its bills without bank support.

The Debt to Worth Ratio indicate that, at all times, creditors' interest in the business was less than the Owner's interest or Net Worth.

We would like to see a larger Net Profit on Sales, but this is a highly competitive line of business. In order to maintain the large volume of business, selling prices must be as low as possible so that Gross Profit margins are also relatively small.

CHAPTER XVI

A Final Special Financial Statement Analysis

Our final "Special" Financial Statement Analysis, and our final, ending Chapter, is another real life factual report and recording of one man's eventual victory over the many dark perils in our Economic Jungle. One wonders what human force drives some men onward directly into the jaws of certain adversity and possible failure. Cervantes' Novel written in 1615, "Don Quixote de la Mancha," seems to be a farcical and impractical fantasy of a man on a horse jousting with Windmills. Don Quixote would aim his slender Lance directly at the whirling blades of a Windmill, urge on his obedient steed, and face certain defeat.

But some other modern men have eagerly grasped the challenge of the whirling blades of the Economic Windmill — and they have emerged bloody, but victorious. Our final Chapter is the true story of another modern "Don Quixote."

In 1945, as the convulsions of World War II were slowly but surely coming to an end, one of the world's largest Corporations, a manufacturer of chemicals, began to look forward to a return to "business as usual." In the hope of developing new products, this giant Corporation sent several of its brightest Chemical Engineers to the small upstate town of Medina, New York. An old unoccupied paper mill was purchased, and those chemical scientists were instructed to experiment with the infusion of certain chemicals into waste cottons and fibrous materials. These experiments were indeed successful and the end product was a revolutionary substitute for natural cow hide leather which was universally used for innersoles in the manufacture of shoes. This new product was not only much less costly than leather, but, in fact, the new material was much more resistant to moisture than leather.

Another very valuable use for the new impregnated fibre was found to be in the manufacture of the common automobile wet-cell battery. Heretofore, cypress wood was the most acceptable and usable material for separating one battery cell from another, and cypress was expensive.

And so it appeared that the giant Chemical Corporation had come up with another winner with its promise of profits to come. However, there suddenly appeared "a fly in the ointment." The United States Justice Department took a dim view of the expansion of the largest Chemical Corporation into so many different and extraneous lines of business and charged "Monopoly and Restraint of Trade" under its Anti-Trust powers. The big Chemical Corporation decided to sell its plant in Medina, New York in order to avoid long, drawn out legal proceedings and harassment. The selling price was $300,000 and included the manufacturing building, machinery and equipment plus the Patents on the substitute leather.

In Cleveland, Ohio, Roger P. Smith heard of this "unusual opportunity." Roger had little experience in the manufacturing process, but had considerable knowledge of and background in Corporate Finance as Treasurer of a medium sized company in Cleveland. Gathering together family and friends, he was able to raise $228,000 in pledges to purchase Capital Stock in his new corporation, R. P. Smith Mfg. Co., Inc. Another $72,000 was desperately needed just to purchase the business alone, not to mention an extra $28,000 for Working Capital after the purchase. Time was of the essence, as other groups of businessmen became interested in the Medina venture.

Then, for Roger, began his first exhausting ordeal in his search for a bank loan of $100,000. He literally flew from city to city talking to commercial bankers, urging, almost pleading for financial help. Everywhere he turned the answer was always the same — "too risky for this size loan." But Roger did not give up, and his determination led him, at the last minute, to a medium sized bank which listened. Based on estimated Net Profits of $20,000 per year, this bank granted the $100,000 loan and Roger had conquered his first obstacle. Yes, the bank took on a real risk, in the **beginning** when it would have been so easy and comfortable to say "No." The "Yes" decision was based on Roger's financial experience and the worthiness of the new product.

In September 1978, R. P. Smith Co., Inc. took over the Medina plant. At once, a variety of new obstacles and problems arose, such

156

as trying to obtain credit for the purchase of raw materials, organizing and expanding a new sales force, setting up a new Chemical Laboratory for product testing and improvement, hiring new key men for plant and manufacturing supervision, and many more.

Our final Analysis covers eighteen years of early struggle and turmoil, gradually ending in complete financial success. The ingredients were a little bit of luck, work, and Determination.

R. P. SMITH CO., INC.

MEDINA, N. Y.

CONDENSED BALANCE SHEET AS OF DECEMBER 31, 1980

ASSETS

Current Assets:

Cash		$ 193,091.18
Accounts receivable		345,186.95
Inventories - at lower of cost or market value:		
Raw materials, supplies, work in process, finished goods and returnable containers		308,259.37
Total Current Assets		846,537.50

Plant Assets:

Land, water rights, buildings and equipment costs	$1,067,766.69	
Less: accumulated depreciation	350,143.85	
Net Recorded Value of Plant Assets		717,622.84
Deferred Charges and Other Assets		11,314.69
TOTAL ASSETS		**$1,575,475.03**

LIABILITIES AND CAPITAL

Current Liabilities:

Notes payable to bank	100,000.00
Accounts payable-trade	171,417.87
Taxes withheld on employees compensation	5,754.29
Employees' welfare fund	127.75
Accrued expenses, wages and commissions	30,833.43
Accrued Federal and State taxes	244,164.00

TOTAL CURRENT LIABILITIES	$ 552,297.34

Capital:

Capital Stock:		
Preferred Stock	198,000.00	
Common Stock	30,000.00	
Total Capital Stock	228,000.00	
Capital Surplus	376,052.79	
Earned Surplus	419,124.90	

TOTAL CAPITAL	1,023,177.69

TOTAL LIABILITIES AND CAPITAL	$1,575,475.03

CONDENSED STATEMENT OF INCOME AND EARNED SURPLUS FOR THE YEAR ENDED DECEMBER 31, 1980

INCOME ACCOUNT

Net Sales	$3,150,299.04
Cost of Goods Sold	2,286,692.49
Gross Profit From Operations	863,606.55
Selling, General and Administrative Expenses and Deductions From Income	440,107.91
Net Income Before Provision For Federal Taxes Based on Income	423,498.64
Provision for Federal Taxes Based on Income	203,305.15
NET INCOME FOR THE YEAR	$ 220,193.49

RECONCILIATION OF EARNED SURPLUS

Earned Surplus, December 31, 1979		$ 208,797.79
Net Income for the Year, as above	$ 220,193.49	
Less: Dividends Paid on Preferred Stock	9,866.38	
Net Increase in Earned Surplus During the Year		210,327.11
Earned Surplus, December 31, 1980		$ 419,124.90

STATEMENT OF FINANCIAL CONDITION

AS OF DECEMBER 31, 1997

Cash	360,663	Accounts Payable	1,323,910
Accounts Receivable	2,030,670	Bank Notes Payable	381,912
Inventory	3,118,165	Income Taxes Payable	696,563
Prepaid Expenses	124,583	Accrued Expenses	350,523
		Mortgage Payments due in 1 Year	530,158
Current Assets	5,634,081	Current Liabilities	3,283,066
Building, Plant and Equipment	4,793,742	Mortgage Payments due after 1 Year	864,222
Other Assets	158,534	Other Deferred Long Term Debt	155,143
		Common Stock	750,000
		Earned Surplus	5,533,296
TOTAL ASSETS	10,586,357	TOTAL LIABILITIES	10,586,357

STATEMENT OF EARNINGS AND RETAINED

EARNINGS AS OF DECEMBER 31, 1997

Net Sales	22,115,579
Cost of Goods Sold	16,694,072
Gross Profit	5,421,507
Expenses, Research, etc.	3,656,613
Net Profit on Sales	1,764,894
Other Expenses	52,288
Income Taxes	878,662
Net Earnings	833,944

RECONCILIATION OF SURPLUS

Surplus Beginning of Year	4,749,982
Add Net Earnings for Year	833,944
Deduct Dividends Paid	50,000
Surplus End of Year	5,533,926

STATEMENT OF FINANCIAL CONDITION

AS OF DECEMBER 31, 1998

Cash	404,320	Bank Notes Payable	1,135,687
Accounts Receivable	2,405,402	Accounts Payable	1,791,803
Inventory	3,862,361	Income Taxes Payable	267,507
Prepaid Expenses	119,456	Accrued Expenses	559,802
		Mortgage Payments due within one year	608,415
Current Assets	6,791,539	Current Liabilities	4,363,214
Building, Plant and Equipment Net	5,848,943	Mortgage Payments due after one year	1,160,487
Other Assets	148,069	Other Deferred Long Term Debt	317,298
		Common Stock	750,000
		Earned Surplus	6,197,552
TOTAL ASSETS	12,788,551	TOTAL LIABILITIES	12,788,551

STATEMENT OF EARNINGS AND RETAINED

EARNINGS AS OF DECEMBER 31, 1988

Net Sales	21,952,279
Cost of Goods Sold	16,634,870
Gross Profit	5,317,409
Expenses, Research, etc.	3,716,507
Net Profit on Sales	1,600,902
Other Expenses	114,998
Net Earnings	1,485,904
Income Taxes	772,278
Net Earnings	713,626

RECONCILIATION OF SURPLUS

Surplus Beginning of Year	5,533,926
Add Net Earnings for Year	713,626
Deduct Dividends Paid	50,000
Surplus End of Year	6,197,552

Now, to the Spread for 1970, 1987, and 1988.

	1980	1987	1988
Current Assets	846,537	5,634,081	6,791,539
Current Liabilities	552,297	3,283,066	4,363,214
Working Capital	294,240	2,351,015	2,428,325
Fixed Assets	728,937	4,952,276	5,997,012
Total Assets	1,575,475	10,586,357	12,788,551
Long Term Debt	—	1,019,365	1,477,785
Net Worth	1,023,177	6,283,926	6,947,552
Sales	3,150,299	22,115,579	21,952,279
Net Profit	220,193	833,944	713,626
Net Worth Gain	—	5,260,749	663,626
		(17 years)	

RATIOS:

	1980	1987	1988
Current Ratio	1.5 to 1	1.7 to 1	1.5 to 1
Liquidity	97%	72%	64%

Debt to Worth	54%	68%	84%
Average Collection Period	39 Days	33 Days	38 Days
Inventory Turnover	10 times	7 times	5.7 times
Net Profit on Sales	7%	3.5%	3.2%

Between 1987 and 1988, Net Worth is Reconciled:

Net Worth 1987 —	$6,283,926
Add Net Profit for 1988 —	713,626
	6,997,552
Deduct Dividends Paid —	50,000
Net Worth End of 1968	6,947,552

Between 1967 and 1968, Working Capital Reconciliation:

Working Capital 1988 —	2,428,325
Working Capital 1987 —	2,351,015
Working Capital Gain —	77,310

Incoming Factors which **Increased** Working Capital:

Net Profit for 1988 —	713,626
Increase in Long Term Loans —	458,420
	1,172,046

Factors which **Decreased** Working Capital:

Increase in Fixed Assets —	1,044,736
Dividends Paid —	50,000
	1,094,736
Increasing Factors —	1,172,046
Decreasing Factors —	1,094,736
Working Capital Gain —	$ 77,310

STATEMENT ANALYSIS

Although the company earned a Net Profit of $713,626 in 1988, Working Capital gained only by $77,310. The answer is found in the "Reconciliation of Working Capital" as additions of $1,044,736 were made to Plant and Machinery below the Line.

Generally, the Analyst prefers to see most of Net Profit retained "above the Line" as an increase in Working Capital. This case is an excellent example of the importance and value of "Reconciliation of Working Capital." We see that not only did the bulk of Net Profit go into Fixed Assets below the Line, but the company borrowed an additional $458,420 in Long Term loans which also were invested in Fixed Assets.

Ordinarily, this heavy increase in investment in Plant and Machinery might be considered an unfavorable trend. Why did management feel it necessary to expand substantially Plant and Machinery?

After several years of continuous increases in Sales year after year, note that Sales in 1988 declined by $163,300 from 1987, and 1988 was an excellent business year for most companies throughout America. The management of R. P. Smith Co., Inc. was faced with a difficult decision. If Sales reached a plateau or declined further, the company would have to reach out for fresh, untapped markets for its products. Therefore, the decision was made to establish a branch factory outside Paris, France, in an effort to capture the European market for substitute leather. This foreign expansion took courage but Sales and Profits were once again on the increase.

Returning to the Financial Statements of 1987 and 1988, the foreign expansion and purchase of substantial Plant and Equipment did not seriously damage the financial condition of R. P. Smith Co., Inc. It is admitted that the Current Ratio of 1.5 to 1 and Liquidity of only 64% are below our preferred standards which we have observed in favorable retail and wholesale Financial Statements. However, a manufacturing company is in an entirely different and special category as the largest Asset, or Investment, must be in Plant Buildings and Machinery.

In 1988, The Smith Company reported almost $6,000,000 in those Fixed Assets as compared to its Net Worth of $6,900,000. Obviously, then, Ratios above the Line, such as the Current Ratio and Liquidity, cannot be expected to be at high levels. Perhaps the most favorable and reassuring Ratio is that Total Debt is 84% of Net Worth. In other words, the owners of Smith Co., Inc. still have the majority interest in their company over creditors.

Net Profit in 1988 of only 3.2% on Sales seems low after all the energy and exertion of creating a Sales Volume of $22,000,000. However, one of the largest Expense items was "Research and Development Costs" for product quality and improvement. Also, note that Net Profit **before** Income Taxes in 1988 was $1,485,904, Income Taxes were $772,278, leaving Net Profit after Taxes of only $713,626.

Of course, this business failure and bankruptcy did not happen overnight. The demise dragged on for three years. The Company was poorly organized as to Capital. But the first year, sales were good and a small profit was earned, so perhaps there was some promise at the start.

But the next year, sales of Ski and Archery Equipment declined sharply and operating losses mounted.

This short Business History ending in failure gives proof to the need for Creditors to demand and insist on Financial Statements each three months and each six months.

The downward trend was visible and failure predictable a year and a half before the End.

INDEX